EDUCATION AND CITIZENSHIP

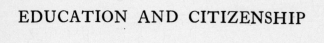

EDUCATION AND CITIZENSHIP

AND OTHER PAPERS

BY

EDWARD KIDDER GRAHAM

LATE PRESIDENT OF THE UNIVERSITY OF NORTH CAROLINA

G. P. PUTNAM'S SONS
NEW YORK AND LONDON
The Knickerbocker Press
1919

The Knickerbocker Press, New York

PREFACE

THE purpose of this volume is to bring together in convenient form and to make easily available a number of the more notable addresses and papers on education, culture, citizenship, and allied subjects, of the late Edward Kidder Graham, President of the University of North Carolina, whose death on October 26, 1918, in his forty-third year, brought his distinguished career as educator and scholar to an untimely end. Owing to the fact that the addresses and papers were intended for special audiences and occasions, and did not receive the careful recasting and revision to which President Graham would have subjected them in preparing such a volume as this, certain repetitions have been inevitable. Similarly, several selections, especially those taken from "The President's Reports" for 1916 and 1917, which are removed from a special setting which cannot be fully explained by the notes accompanying them, may seem to begin and end too abruptly for inclusion here. These defects, however, are so slight in comparison with the total impression conveyed by the papers, that they can easily be overlooked. All the papers included in the volume have appeared in magazines or other publications, and definite acknowledgments are hereinafter made at the appropriate places. To Professor H. W. Chase, Chairman of the Faculty, and Professor Edwin Greenlaw, of the Department of English, I am indebted for assistance in preparing the volume for the press.

LOUIS R. WILSON.

CHAPEL HILL, N. C.

CONTENTS

I

EDUCATION AND DEMOCRACY

II

CULTURE AND CITIZENSHIP

III

STUDENT AND COLLEGE RELAT ONS

Contents

INTRODUCTION

EDWARD KIDDER GRAHAM began and ended the
work of his life during the first two decades of the
twentieth century. Within this short period, by
the might of clear thinking and unselfish devotion,
he won enduring fame as a scholar and writer of
originality and quiet grace, as a teacher of sympathetic and stimulating quality, as an executive
of unforgetable genius for inspiration and coöperation, and as an interpreter of democracy modified by
culture and training, of rare and singular strength.
This is a great total of achievement for a man of
fragile physical mold burdened from the outset
with heavy daily tasks and ever-increasing cares
and responsibilities, and reveals a personality
worthy of the study of those who pin their faith
to a social order whose ultimate claim to lasting
validity must rest perforce upon self-discipline
and the perfectibility of the individual.

Graham was fortunate in the stock from which
he sprang, the era in which he grew to manhood,
and the mood of the society which helped in some
measure to fashion his ideals and impulses. Between 1876, the year in which he was born, and
1899, the year in which he entered upon the work

of his life, the State of North Carolina and the
states of the South generally, finally triumphed
over the ruin and exhaustion of war, and found a
way to industrialize their society and to modern-
ize their spirit without commercializing their
souls. They clung to their older traditions of
simplicity and personality, but contrived to fasten
upon community effort and civic progress as the
foundation stones of a new national development.
Like all bruised and broken peoples they were
beginning to turn with constructive purpose to the
younger generation for the realization of their
hopes and dreams.

There was a fine seriousness in the air of the
time, a noble conception of public probity, a clear
call to youth to realize its highest self in the temper
of the modern world and if need be to spend itself
for the common welfare. Edward Graham heard
and heeded this call even in his undergraduate
days. It so fell out that he and I came together
more intimately than is usually the case between
student and president. We walked and talked
together, and I found myself quite naturally taking
counsel of him and debating with him the American scene as it then lay before us. There was always
some unrevealed force about him that intrigued
the imagination and invested his simplicity and
unpretentiousness with a very potent charm.

The crude and obvious ambition of a merely
talented youth did not fret or absorb him. He did

not pose about anything, and there was no striving after the status of the intellectual or the reputation of the Admirable Crichton in his career. But when one had reason to call to mind the reliable, outstanding youths in the body of 'students, there always emerged the alert, quietly-humorous, keen-eyed, right-minded, reflective face and figure of this self-reliant young man. Earlier than most men, even of genius, he learned to respect his mind and to use it sternly and reverently. His mind to him a kingdom was, with a sovereignty to safe-guard and severe conflict to endure from which it must not "blench or withdraw."

The literary style of Graham, reflecting always a certain quaintness and playfulness, gains its strength and felicity largely from the vigor and in-tegrity of his thinking, rather than from any heat of passion or imaginative excess. He used his brain to think with, and, as a sort of matter of intel-lectual conscience, kept it ready for instant test.

The word culture was, next to democracy, often-est upon his lips, and I am convinced that the innermost urging of his life was to comprehend completely these two great postulates and to relate them to each other so that there would issue in the contacts of common life about him a vitalized culture and a humanized democracy. Some men are born with the instinct of culture, and Graham was such a man. Instinctive association or apti-tude for the lasting and classic and symmetrical expression—whether in the field of ethics or taste or art or reasoning—inhered in the man's nature.

The same infallible instincts invigorated by severe thought led him to his high interpretation of democracy. This great optimism which now flies its flag over a world redeemed by its valor and toughness and faith was not to him a mere political or philosophical slogan. It was a religion, a spirit, a principle of life and service. His orderly mind had long since established the kinship and interdependence between education and democracy, and his flaming spirit had admonished him that they must be made to know each other better and serve each other better.

There could not have been found a better platform or sounding board from which to conduct his operations and preach his policy of education and life than the University of North Carolina. It was an ancient State University, saturated with a practical democratic atmosphere, capable of sustained enthusiasms, of steadfast aims, institutional unselfishness, and buoyant hope. A serene good fortune lifted him to the presidency of this institution, which he loved as if it were made of flesh and blood, in the prime of life and at the moment when a war of liberation from outworn tyrannies burst upon the world, releasing all men's energies and heightening and purifying all men's spirits. With a vision clear and far-reaching, a patience that was

Introduction

boundless, a sympathy that knew no limits, a
steely energy that relaxed only to spring into
greater strength, he adventured upon the task of
tying together in one whole fabric the needs of the
people and the resources of learning. The methods
he used were as diverse and varied as the problem
he sought to solve. Like Cardinal Newman he
flung himself again and again at the task of defining and analyzing the functions of universities
and democracies; and the papers in this volume
illustrate the clarity and beauty of these defini-
tions, as well as the intensity of feeling that drove
him onward to his goal. But he was too wise to
neglect the pragmatical and practical or to slight
the technical and scholarly aspects of the problem.
And so the University grew in scientific authority
as well as in social approach.

The story of educational progress among self-
governing peoples is full of similar struggles for the
lifting of theory and practice to higher levels, but I
know of none swifter and finer and more fruitful
than Graham's struggle for the complete sociali-
zation of an ancient State University in the tense
quadrennium of the World War. The love and
confidence of his colleagues and students, the affection of a great conservative commonwealth, not
given to heady loyalties, attested to the completeness of his success. When death came to still his
dauntless heart, I fancy he was not denied the
power, through faith, to see the vision of victory

everywhere about him—victory for his cherished purposes, victory for the forces of freedom in the wide world, and victory in his own soul.

EDWIN A. ALDERMAN.

CHARLOTTESVILLE, VA.

I

EDUCATION AND DEMOCRACY

INAUGURAL ADDRESS[1]

THIS high commission I receive from the State in a spirit of deep and reverent confidence that does not spring from any thought of personal resource. If all of the wealth of treasured memory and hope that this institution represents were an individual responsibility, it would be a burden too heavy to be borne; but this great company of her sons, and her kindred, and her friends is testimony to the wide and loyal fellowship of learning that hedges her securely round about, and makes the individual heart strong enough for anything. Nor less reassuring, as the standard passes to an untried hand, is the host of happy thoughts released by the presence of those who since the reopening gave themselves to her guidance in wisdom and complete devotion. To them to-day the institution pays the perfect tribute of her abundant life that they gave their strength to promote: to her latest leader, the architect of her material rebuilding, whose wise and patient care inwrought into her standard the ideals of modern scholarship; to his predecessor, whose sympa-

[1] As president of the University of North Carolina, April 21, 1915.

3

thetic insight and statesmanlike vision gave eloquent expression to the voiceless aspiration of his
people and made him their interpreter, both to
themselves and to the nation; to his predecessor,
whose aggressive and brilliant leadership performed
the essential service of making the University a
popular right and privilege; to his predecessor—
the historian of her heroic past, on whose heart
each syllable of her story is written—who lived
through a period of bitterness without a hate, who
endured poverty without a regret, achieved honor
without pride, and who now so deeply shares the
eternal youth about him that age finds him with
a heart so young and a life so full of affection and
praise that he is the witness of his own immortality.

As the mind dwells on all of this exalted loyalty
and unselfish devotion, once again persons, even
the most heroic, fade into the background of the
cause that evoked their heroisms, and our present
ceremonial becomes less the installation of an
individual than a reverent and passionate dedica-
tion of all of us and all of the energies and powers
of all of us to the civilization that the institution
exists to serve.

The life of this institution began with the life
of the nation itself; and the period since its rebirth
in 1875 is the great period of national construction.   In these forty years the nation was caught
up in the giant's swing of its material release, and
through the exploitation and development of its

natural resources, through immigration, invention, industrial combination, and commercial expansion constructed a civilization startling and wonderful in the things it fashioned, in the type of constructive genius it elicited, in the new tyrannies and ideals it evolved. In this notable half-century, all America became, in the summarizing phrase of Mr. Wells, "one tremendous escape from ancient obsessions into activity and making." Its liberated energies drew from the wealth of the continent material achievements and qualities of a sort unmatched in the history of civilization, through which it became, in its own brave acclaim of conquest and creation, "triumphant democracy."

The section that this institution served was only partly affected by this great expansion; but for it, too, the period is more than anything else a period of construction and making. In the last ten years of the existence of this institution before the war, the wealth of the South was about one half that of the whole country. In these ten years, its wealth increased one billion dollars more than that of New England and the Middle States combined. In 1875, when the University began its life over again, the whole South was bankrupt.

In these forty years of material rebuilding it too has escaped from ancient obsessions not a few, and has won, in patience and fortitude under the austere discipline of a fierce, unequal struggle, not only the spiritual compensations of the struggle,

but material liberation that is not a promise but
an immediate reality. And while it is under the
thrill of the prosperity within its grasp, it is not
primarily because in the past ten years its bank
deposits and the capital invested in its manufactures have increased tenfold, that half of the
nation's exports originate in its ports, that a world
treasure hidden in its oil, gas, coal, iron, water-
power, and agriculture makes certain the fact that
the next great expansion in national life will be
here, and that here will be "the focusing point of
the world's commerce"; the summons that puts
the eager and prophetic tone in Southern life to-day
is the consciousness that here under circumstances
pregnant with happy destiny men will make once
more the experiment of translating prosperity in
terms of a great civilization. It is to leadership
in this supreme adventure of democratic commonwealth building that the universities of the South
are called, and their real achievements depend
upon the sure intelligence, sympathy, and power,
with which they perform their vital function, and
make authoritative answer to the compelling question of the people as to what, if anything, in the
way of clear guidance they have to offer, or must
we look to another?

An institution to express and minister to the
highest aspirations of man was an immediate provision of the founders of the first states of the
new republic. It was the organic law of part a

of North Carolina, and the University of North
Carolina was the first of the state universities to
be chartered, followed quickly by those of Georgia
and South Carolina. They were fostered, however, not by the whole people, but by groups of
devoted men who sought to have them perform
for the new country the noble service of the historic
colleges of the old. It was the author of the Declaration of Independence who by faith saw in the
new country a new civilization with a new philosophy, and who saw implicit in that a new institution for its realization. Jefferson sought to create
in the university of the state an institution that
would not only through traditional culture values
give to the state "legislators, and judges . . . and
expound the principles and structure of government," but would also "harmonize and promote
the interests of agriculture, manufacture, and
commerce, and by well-formed views of political
economy give free course to public industry."
To the traditional models then existent he advocated an institution that would meet all the needs
of all of the state, and to this end planned courses
in manual training, engineering, agriculture, horti-
culture, military training, veterinary surgery, and
for schools of commerce, manufacturing, and diplomacy, and in the details of its administration
he planned to keep it flexible and responsive to
the people's need.

But in spite of this splendid program the state

university could not come into its own in the South, nor for a hundred years be realized anywhere. The great American idea that Jefferson conceived had to wait until America itself could come into being, and the mission of interpretative leadership passed to other hands, as the section which gave it birth lost contact with the spirit of national life.

The evolution of the American state university during the past hundred years is the record of the gradual fulfilling of Jefferson's splendid vision. It represents the vital history of the contribution of nineteenth-century America to the progress of mankind. The diffusion of wealth and knowledge, geographical and scientific discovery, new inventions and new ideals, not only put a power and a passion into material making and construction, but they fashioned institutions of training in whatever vocation the all-conquering hand of materialism demanded, and these as they developed were added to those that other civilizations had created. To the institutions that seek to express man's inner life and his relations to the past and the fixity of those relations, it added institutions that interpret his outer life, his relation to the present and his infinite capacity for progress. It seeks to reassert for present civilization what past civilizations say to America, together with what America has to say for itself. Through its colleges of liberal arts, pure and applied science, professional and technical schools it repeats the culture messages of the prophets of the nineteenth century: Arnold's message of sweetness and light; Huxley's message of the spirit of inquiry, and Carlyle's message of the spirit of work.

In this grouping, then, of the college of culture, the college of research, the college of vocation into a compartmental organization of efficient and specialized parts, supplemented by the idea of centering its energy and ingenuity in putting all of its resources directly at the service of all the people—is this the ultimate thought of this greatest institution of the modern state, and is its future to be concerned merely with perfecting these parts and further extending their utility?

Culture as learning, science as investigation, and work as utility, each has an eternal life of its own, and to perfect each of them for the performance of its special work will always be an aim of the University. But this conception of its function as a university is necessarily partial and transitional. Tyndall, in his great Belfast address, made in 1874, points out that it is not through science, nor through literature that human nature is made whole, but through a fusion of both. Through its attempt to make a new fusion of both with work during the great constructive years of the past half-century, our civilization has caught the impulse of a new culture center.

It is this that the state university seeks to express. It is more than an aggregate of parts. As a university it is a living unity, an organism at the heart of the living democratic state, interpreting its life, not by parts, or by a summary of parts, but wholly—fusing the functions of brain and heart and hand under the power of the immortal spirit of democracy as it moves in present American life to the complete realization of what men really want. The real measure of its power will be whether, discarding the irrelevancies of the past and present, it can focus, fuse, and interpret their eternal verities and radiate them from a new organic center of culture. This, let it tentatively define as achievement touched by fine feeling— as truth alive and at work in the world of men and things.

Such new centers are the vital source of civilization, and the propulsive power of progress. Every now and then in human history men make a synthesis of their ideals, giving redirection and increased projection to their energies on new and higher levels of achievement. Truly great creative periods thus result from the liberation of men through new revelations of deeper and richer values in their new relations. Classical learning gave Europe such a period in the Renaissance; science gave the modern world such a period, each expressing itself through a great educational institution, typifying the union of past ideals into a new center of reality. The American state university of the twentieth century is an organism of the productive state, striving to express in tangible realities the aspirations of present democracy, as it adjusts itself to the liberations of a new humanism.

The evolution of the democratic state in the past hundred years as an attempt to actualize in human society the principles of liberty, equality, and brotherhood is parallel to that of the state university. Traditional ideals and institutions it, too, inherited that it could not willfully discard; new ideals it, too, aspired to that it could not immediately achieve. Its continental task of "construction and making" made the production of material values its necessary concern. The incarnation of the great anti-feudal power of commerce was inevitable, not only to break the bonds of the "ancient obsessions," but to open through its material might railways, steamship lines, canals, telegraph and telephone systems, good roads, schoolhouses and libraries, as avenues to liberation. In its development it created its own abnormal standards and tyrannies, and became so obsessed with material freedom that equality seemed a contradiction and coöperation the vision of a dreamer. Its life was individualistic, compartmental, and fiercely competitive. Its ideal was efficiency; its criterion, dividends; but present democracy, if it has not yet focused

the light to the new center toward which it moves,
is steadily illumined by it. Democracy has come
to mean more than an aggregate of vocations,
grouped for the purpose of material exploitation.
The whole effort of the productive state is to
unify its life, not by casting out material good,
but by interpreting and using it in its symmetrical
upbuilding.

Great progress toward making the state a co-
operative organism in the equal distribution of all
the elements of life to all according to their capacity, has been made in the evolution of business
itself. "Business is business" is no longer its
ultimate thought. In perfecting its parts for efficiency it discovered, not merely the value of
coöperation in the individual business, but in the
larger aggregates of material expansion that the
coöperation of manufactures, commerce, and agriculture is necessary to prosperity, and that the
weakness of one is the weakness of all. It has
come to see in addition to this extensive unity
an intensive unity in its dependence on knowledge, science, and ethics; and more deeply still
that the organic center of all of its actions and
interactions for liberating its efficiency and its
life to a higher level of productivity is in raising
the productivity of all of the men engaged in it
by liberating all of their wholesome faculties.
Scientific management, which will in the present
century mark as great progress in production as

the introduction of machinery did in the past century, shifts the main emphasis of production from the machine to the worker. The new freedom in whatever form—in business, politics, religion, and philosophy—is a manifestation of the effort of democracy to establish the supremacy of human values, and so to make of itself the creative, spiritual organism it must be. From this new center of constructive coöperation, it is already in its effort to abolish ignorance, poverty, disease, and crime, sending confident premonitions of fuller life and new and braver reconstructions. The productive democratic state would make of itself an organism, by making its compartmental life a union of all of its parts, as the nation made of the states a territorial union. It would perfect the parts through the stronger, fuller life of the whole; it would lose none of the good of individual initiative and material success, but would translate it all into the whole term of higher human values. It cries with the creative joy of spent life renewed:

> All good things are ours,
> Nor soul helps flesh more
> Than flesh helps soul.

The state university is the instrument of democracy for realizing all of these high and healthful aspirations of the state. Creating and procreated by the state it has no immediate part, however, in a specific social program. Its service is deeper and more pervasive. It sees its problem as positive, not negative; as one of fundamental health, not of superficial disease. It looks on the state as a producer; not as a policeman. It is not so much concerned with doing a certain set of things, as infusing the way of doing all things with a certain ideal. Not by spasmodic reform, nor by sentiment, nor by the expiations of philanthropy; but by understanding, criticism, research and applied knowledge it would reveal the unity of the channels through which life flows, and minister to the purification of its currents. It would conceive the present state and all of its practical problems as the field of its service, but it would free the term service from the narrowing construction of immediate practice. The whole function of education is to make straight and clear the way for the liberation of the spirit of men from the tyranny of place and time, not by running away from the world, but by mastering it. The university would hold to the truth of practical education that no knowledge is worth while that is not related to the present life of man; it would reject its error that only knowledge of nearby things has such a relation; it would hold to the truth of classical education (I quote) that "things high and far away often bestow best control over things that are detailed and

near," and reject its error of concluding that
because certain things are high and distant they
must possess that power. It would emphasize
the fact that research and classical culture rightly
interpreted are as deeply and completely service
as any vocational service; but it would consider
their service too precious to be confined in clois-
ters and sufficiently robust to inhabit the walks
of men. The whole value of university extension
depends upon the validity of the purity and power
of the spirit of the truth from which it is derived.
Extension it would interpret, not as thinly stretch-
ing out its resources to the state boundaries for
the purposes of protective popularity, or as carrying down to those without the castle gates broken
bits of learning, but as the radiating power of a
new passion, carrying in natural circulation the
unified culture of the race to all parts of the body
politic. It would interpret its service, not as
sacrifice, but as life, the normal functioning of
life as fruitful and fundamental as the relation
between the vine and the branches.

It is this organic relation to the democratic
state that puts the southern state university at
the vital center of the state's formative material
prosperity. "What are southern universities doing," asks a great industrial leader, "to give
economic independence to southern industry?"
It is a fair challenge, and the state university
joyfully acknowledges its obligation fully to meet

it.   It is a part of the business of laboratories to function in the productive state by solving the problems of embarrassed industry.   Science has so faithfully performed this obligation that the main arch of modern industry rests on the laboratory.   Applied science no less truly rests on pure science and the liberating currents of the spirit of inquiry and investigation that is the vital spark of modern life.   The first great step in the independence of southern industry will be the realization of its dependence.   Our whole electrical power liberation, significant now in achievement and thrilling in prophecy, is the coöperation of a hundred forces, the most important of which is the vital force of unknown investigators whose labor and spirit opened the current to the wheels of productive industry.   Says Walter Bagehot:

If it had not been for quiet people who sat still and studied the sections of the cone, if other quiet people had not sat still and worked out the doctrine of chances . . . ; if star gazers had not watched long and carefully the motions of the heavenly bodies, our modern astronomy would have been impossible, and without our astronomy, our ships, our colonies, our seamen, and all that makes modern life could not have existed.

The aniline industry of Germany is not the product of the clever alchemy of a laboratory merely.   It is the logical result of a great state

replacing through its university "by intellectual
forces the physical forces lost by war." It is the
result, too, of the fusion with this of industrial
statesmanship; the result of a mastery of industry's extensive and intensive relations in economic
law, foreign commerce, science, and diplomacy.
Says the Secretary of Commerce:

Foreign trade begins inside a man's head, in the
shape of knowledge of the country to which he would
sell—its customs, finances, language, weights, measures, and business methods.

The state university would make clear the fact
that in its relation to southern industry, while it
regards every practical need as an opportunity
for service, its still larger service is in making
clear the relations that radiate from industry in
concentric fields of knowledge that either enslave
it if they are not understood, or liberate it in ever
increasing life and power if they are understood.
And their chief liberation is the setting free of the
master of industry himself. All industry that is
worthy of absorbing a man's life is in the grasp of
the world relations and under the grim test of
world standards. Any work that does evoke a
man's full faculties in mastering its relations is
worthy work. So it is the function of the University, not merely to bring its resources to bear in
solving practical problems of industry and dis-

covering through its inner relations the field
of southern industry as a field of statesmanship,
but in discovering thereby the further truth that
in perfecting its relations it becomes a liberal
vocation in saving the man and all of his higher
faculties, not from business, but through business.
Salvation will come there or nowhere. The question for southern industry is whether in the world
opportunity that opens ahead, it will attempt
the futile experiment of becoming big through
superficial and selfish efficiency, or whether, through
a mastery of all of its relations, while becoming
big it will also become great.

One of the belated visions of southern business
and educational statesmanship is that we can have
here no full prosperity or civilization unless agriculture is made truly productive. In our individualistic, political, and economic life we have
flattered it, ignored it, or exploited it. We have
lately awakened to the fact that it is an almost
dead center at the heart of southern progress, and
we have had the vision that it is our function to
coöperate with it fully and wholly. It is inevitable that society's need will make farming efficient
as a business. In bringing this about one of two
processes is possible: that it be developed as other
great businesses are, with routine skilled labor
under captains of industry; or that it be made a
liberal human vocation, each farm home the center of a whole and wholesome life, and perfecting

the development of a definite and complete civilization. What will make it realize its higher destiny will not be a limited view of it as a manual vocation. It is a manual vocation, and as such should be trained to the highest human efficiency as a producer of wealth. It must be more deeply interpreted, however, if it is to attract and hold men of energy and initiative. In its relation to nature, to the applied sciences, to economics, and the social sciences agriculture has relations that put it on the full current of the forces that make for human culture through right relations to it as work by evoking, not only prosperity from the soil, but the higher faculties of the man himself—making of the cropper, the farmer; and of the farmer, man-on-the-farm.

The reality of the state university's power to liberate the faculties and aspirations of the workers in the productive state depends on the force of that power as generated in it as an association of teachers and students, given wholly to the pursuit of truth and free from the distractions of making a living. The heart of this association, the college of liberal arts and sciences, has as its mission now as always the revelation of the full meaning of life in its broad and general relations, and to fix in the heart of its youth a point of outlook on the field of human endeavor from which to see it clearly and to see it whole. It fears no criticism based on an interpretation of its mission

as "impractical"; but it does regard as fatal any
failure to evoke the best powers of its own student
body. President Wilson has spoken of present
undergraduate life as "a non-conducting medium"
of intellectual discipline, and President Pritchett
sums up all possible condemnation when he says
that it is an organization where conditions within
are such that success in the things for which it
stands no longer appeals to those within it. Failure to appeal may not be laid to the curriculum
nor to the spirit of youth nor to the spirit of the
age. "The things for which it stands" in the
mastery of fact, the mastery of method, and in
spiritual tone will come not because they are
latent in Greek or in physics; but because they
are made luminous there through a revelation of
the broad and liberal relations of these studies to
the life curiosities of the student. A course in
Greek may be as narrowing and as blighting
to a thirsty spirit as a dissertation in medieval
theology; a liberal arts curriculum at its conclusion
may be in the mind of the young graduate not
more impressively unified and tangible than the
wreckage of a once passionate contest between
literature and science. The line of memory and
repetition is the line of least resistance to student
and teacher as it is in the dead routine of every
field of effort; but the liberal arts course is not
a mechanical contrivance for standardizing the
crude material fed to it. It is the life history of

the human spirit and its wonderful adventures in the world, unrolled to the eye of aspiring youth setting out on its wonderful adventure. For this great business of touching the imagination and stirring the soul to original activity, no formulas nor technique, however conscientious, will serve. For liberal training to make its connections, eager, sympathetic interpretation is necessary, "with thought like an edge of steel and desire like a flame." From the center of every subject runs the vital current of its inner meaning, and from all subjects in the curriculum in converging lines to the heart of our present civilization and its culture message. Intellectual discipline, special insights, and "success in the thing for which it stands" will appeal to those within, not by means of new subjects added with the thought of gaining interest nor by repeating the assertion that the old subjects ought to have cultural appeal; but by having the thing for which it stands radiantly and constantly clear to itself and the touchstone of its activities. It is the incarnation in the individual of the spirit of the institution as it focuses and reflects the inmost message of the age. This is the source of the student's special insights, his scent for reality, and their fruitage is that productive thinking that is the supreme test of the college.

The association of teacher and student in the professional schools must have the same unifying point of view. Widely separated as the profes-

sional schools are in subject-matter, they have
not only a common scientific method and spirit
in their pursuit, but a common culture center in
their larger human relations. Arnold conceived
of the professional training given at Cornell in the
making of engineers and architects as an illustration of what culture is not. The criterion of
the American state university is not a matter of
the vocation, but whether in making the student
efficient in his vocation it has focused through his
studies its own inner light so as to liberalize him
as a member of democratic society. It is not the
function of the university to make a man clever
in his profession merely. That is a comparatively
easy and negligible university task. It is also
to make vivid to him through his profession his
deeper relations—not merely proficiency in making a good living, but productivity in living a
whole life. The professions of law, medicine, the
ministry, journalism, commerce, and the rest are
essential to the upbuilding of a democratic commonwealth; but they must be interpreted, not
as adventures in selfish advancement, but as
enterprises in constructive statesmanship, liberating both the state and the man. It is the function
of the university, not only to train men in the
technique of law, but to lift them to a higher level
of achievement by making them living epistles
of social justice; not only to make clever practi-
tioners of medicine, but to lift them into conser-

vators of the public health; not merely to train teachers in the facts and the methods of education, but to fire them with the conviction that they are the productive creators of a new civilization.

It recognizes no antagonist in this general business but ignorance. Ignorance it conceives as the unpardonable sin of a democracy and on it in every form it would wage relentless warfare. To this end it would unify and coördinate its whole system of public education in a spiritual union of elementary schools and secondary schools, of agricultural and mechanical and normal colleges, of private and denominational schools and colleges, all as a means to the end of the great commonwealth for which men have dreamed and died but scarcely dared to hope. Fully conscious of the confusions of prejudice and the blind unreason of self-interest and greed, it is even more conscious of the curative powers of the democratic state and its indomitable purpose to be wholly free. So it would enlist all vocations and all professions in a comprehensive, state-wide program of achieving as a practical reality Burke's conception of the state as "a partnership in all science, a partnership in all art, a partnership in every virtue and in all perfection, and since such a partnership cannot be attained in one generation, a partnership between all those who are living, and those who are dead, and those who are yet unborn."

This is the understanding of the meaning of

life which represents the highest level to which men of our civilization have attained—the highest good at which the state aims. The religious perception of our time in its widest application is the consciousness that our well-being, both material and spiritual, lies in intelligent coöperation. The state university in its sympathetic study of relations that reconcile the divisions of society, while not concerned with differences in religious organization is inevitably and profoundly concerned with religion itself. All of its study of men and things leads through the coöperating channels that connect them beyond the sources of immediate life to the one great unity that binds all together. The human mind, whatever its achievement, in whatever fields of endeavor, "with the yearning of a pilgrim for its home, will still turn to the mystery from which it emerged, seeking to give unity to work and thought and faith." The state university in its passionate effort to fashion this unity into a commonwealth of truly noble proportions of work and worth and worship, reverently prays as it follows the star of its faith: "Oh God, I think Thy thoughts after Thee."

Such is the covenant of our immortal mother "with those who are living and those who are dead and those who are yet unborn," "building herself from immemorial time as each generation kneels and fights and fades." She will hold secure her priceless heritage from her elder sons as the

pledge of the faith she keeps; and she will cherish
the passionate loyalty of her latest issue with the
sacred pride that only a mother knows; she will
seek guidance above the confusion of voices that
cry out paths of duty around her, in the experience
of the great of her kind the world over; but she
will not, in self-contemplation and imitation, lose
her own creative power and that original genius
that alone gives her value in the world. As the
alma mater of the living state and all of its higher
aspirations she would draw from it the strength
that is as the strength of its everlasting hills and
give answer in terms of whole and wholesome life
as fresh as the winds of the world that draw new
life from its pine-clad plains. Eager, sympathetic,
unafraid, and with the understanding heart "she
standeth on the top of the high places, by the way
in the places of the path; she crieth out at the
entry of the city, at the coming in at the doors:
'Unto you, O men, I call and my voice is to the
sons of men.' "

THE AMERICAN UNIVERSITY AND THE NEW NATIONALISM[1]

A CAMBRIDGE graduate, at the front, in a letter to one of the Masters, writes: "Don't trouble to say anything about the war. I know all that is to be said about that; let me hear what, if anything, is happening at Cambridge; that the old place is there, at all events."

Something of this feeling of its not being necessary to say anything about the war, we are coming to share. With a growing consciousness of the size of the concrete task to be performed, and the finding of our effective place in intelligent action, talk becomes trivial, and prophecy as to what must come in the way of reconstruction almost disloyal to the immediate imperative. We have been forced to grasp the grim fact that, when poison gas and shrapnel take the place of sweetness and light, the chief end of men who would glorify God is to kill Germans—and no explanatory footnotes required.

And yet what, if anything, is to be told about

[1] A Commencement Address intended (but undelivered on account of illness) for Johns Hopkins University, June, 1918, and published in *The Johns Hopkins University Circular* for July.

the "happenings at Cambridge" must be told in
terms of war, and of the effect that this supreme
fact in present and future human experience is
having on all institutions that truly interpret life
to living men; at all events if the old places are
still to be *there* in any more vital sense than as a
precious reminiscence. So my theme to-day of
the relation of the war to American institutions
of higher learning is inevitable, and, just now, so
important and fundamental that I can only wish
a voice more authoritative than mine might say
what we are all coming to feel. For, far from the
present emergency being a period of academic
suspense when the actual business in hand must
be left to what are known as "practical men,"
the acutely clear thing is that the supreme opportunity of the American university inheres in the
fact that it is, more than any other, in its nature,
the institution to answer the nation's present need.

The directly practical response of the college
to the need of the nation in the past year of the
war was immediate and convincing. Its under-
graduates and young alumni showed an instant
and instinctive readiness to volunteer for any
service, and a capacity for specialized service, as
officers and otherwise, that was nowhere else
available. The fact that the number of students
in American colleges this year is 68,000 less than
it was last, shows only to a limited degree the
whole-hearted spirit with which college students

answered the first war call for the raw material
of man-power. The only limit to their readiness
to enlist for direct service was the desire of the
Government that they continue their college
training as long as possible.

In this the Government has wisely recognized
the fact that the college has a higher utility than
furnishing physical man-power. Modern warfare
has made terribly clear the unique service of the
college in multiplying the physical power of a man
through giving him a mastery of organized applied
knowledge. A nation's fighting force, if it does
not have behind it the power of the sciences, for
which the college is the training camp, is as im-
potent as a cave man's club against a Browning
gun. The modern battle front is truly seen as
organized, mobilized ideas in action. Behind
each individual man is the miraculous wealth of
power that all of the sciences, through their upgrowth in the past century, have been able to
discover, coördinate, and utilize in tools and
machines of construction and destruction. Physics, chemistry, medicine, engineering—the whole
range of the pure and applied sciences—are the
epic heroes in a war that summarizes the life
interests of over a billion people. It is this vast
mass of human beings, brought into ever closer
and closer relationships through science, and it is
the infinite momentum of the power of their
mobilized ideas, that speaks in battles for which

history furnishes no parallel. At Verdun, the French alone used 6,000,000 shells, containing 1,800,000 tons of steel.

The business of living and fighting was simpler in the days when David, representing the easy freedom of his pastoral tribe—with his scrip and staff, and with his sling and "five smooth stones" —faced Goliath of Gath across the valley of Elah. The difference between the individual prowess of those ancient warriors and the individual physical prowess of the men who faced each other at the Marne, is not great. The progress of the civilization that stretches between is in the ideas that men have been able to subdue to their use in the conquest of the hidden forces of earth and sea and sky, and in the mastery of the growingly tense and difficult enterprise of living together. The college, in this essential field of organized ideas, peculiarly its own, through its laboratories and lecture rooms, its investigators and teachers, its expert service, its specially trained graduates, has been suddenly and almost sensationally discovered by the war to be the central agency of civilization.

But there is a far deeper and more inspiring revelation that has come to the college as a social institution in the service of the nation for the mobilization of material and men through ideas, than is represented by the stars in its service flag and by its organized and applied science. There is a mobilization deeper than materials

and machines, on which all vital organization
depends,—"Strength and direction of the convictions of men—formulated as loyalties—furnish
the decisive motive power of a nation's energies."
The living spring, the soul, of vital mobilization,
is what, in our commonplace war vocabulary, we
call *morale*. When young David went out to
fight for the civilization of Israel, it was not merely
on his sling and those "five smooth pebbles" that
he relied. What made that improvised weapon
and that beautiful young strength of his sufficient
for the task was that in his mind and heart was
the coördinate faith of his people. Men and
material and applied ideas are not separate parts
of an assembled machine that can merely *do*
something; they are functional parts of a living
organism that also *believes* something. "Thou
comest to me," said young David to Goliath,
"with a sword and with a shield, and I come to
thee in the name of the Lord of hosts, and the
God of the armies of Israel."

In the midst of the first impact of the necessity
for accomplishing a task too colossal in its practical
nature quickly to grasp, what has come to the
nation as a whole during the past twelve months
is this greatest human experience: As it summoned its powers to *do* something, it discovered
that it *believes* something,—a faith sufficient for
the task. As the country gradually caught the
rhythm of its marching men,—following the bitter,

silent period of national hesitation,—unified from the apparent racial, industrial, spiritual confusion of a Kitchener's mob, its first experience was an exhilarating, even thrilling, sense of power released in decision. And then, in the silent fashion of deep and simple things, came the conviction that this power has its source in the fellowship of an invincible national faith. This is the message that one hears from the man on the street, and in the smoking-car and store and factory, as well as from the pulpit and press and campus. America has a faith, as a nation, she means to interpret in terms of a better sort of living for men.

What has happened to the nation, as it has come (or is now coming) to itself, is not unlike what we of the colleges saw happen to our young college men when they left the campus for the military training camps. They left us restless irresponsibles whose miscellaneous inactivities had been our despair, and after three months they came back, and we were happily astonished to find them new men,—mobilized, physically and mentally, into *whole* men of almost super-accomplishment through the inspiration of a new clear purpose that shone through confident eyes. To them "there was a new sort of health and utility; of things desperately moving and interesting, and the wonderful surprise of finding themselves equal to anything." Life had broken through the old traps of fixed conventions and habits; and for the privileges and comforts to be given up there was a glad abundant faith for the hazards of the open road.

Maurice Barrès, of the French Academy, properly considers this new spirit of youthful faith, liberated through the war, important enough to appraise, and prints a collection of letters from young Frenchmen, who died in battle: "Our sacrifices will be sweet," writes one of nineteen years, "if there should be more light for the souls of men; if truth shall come forth more radiant and better beloved."—"Loyalty, love, liberty, honor, these," writes another, "are to me no meaningless phrases. They ring like a bugle in my young heart, and when the moment comes I shall make the supreme sacrifice."—"I believe in Beauty, Youth, in Life. I believe in God, in France, in Victory!" Letters from American youth, and young Englishmen and Canadians, are not in this exalted key, naturally lacking the radiant French passion for nationalism; but the same reality of freshly discovered faith is there, however suppressed. "This is hellish business, first and last," writes one; "I would not be anywhere else for the world."—"Sometimes the thought of why we are learning these things strikes me like a blow in the face, and it is hard to realize that they must have a place in the building up of the world. Knowledge of how to kill is not pleasant, but must result in clearing up the ground

for the great temple that is to come."—"My eyes
are opened to the fact that I am a part of the
biggest thing that ever happened in human experience. I gladly give up all my personal ambitions
to contribute to the great result." It is not a
question, here, of argument, excitement, or even
conscious duty or honor. It is something stronger
and finer,—a passion for that citizenship in the
world that is sportsmanship in the large, and
humanity in the largest sense, that instead of
growing dim and faint in long peace and prosperity
seems to have the freshness and spontaneity of
elemental life itself. Yesterday, these were meaningless phrases to a cynical world that in slavery
to its habitual conventions had learned the
price-tags of everything, and had half-forgotten its
standard of human values; to-day, they ring like
a bugle call to the young heart of the world, certi-
fied as the living faith of men who willingly die
for them as the only realities. This is the instinctive spirit of our youth and of the young nation,
and the faith of our youngest graduate will re-
discover to our most ancient foundation the truth
that its supreme function is vitally to interpret
the indomitable impulse of men to be master of
all good things that their work and skill have
produced, in order to be free,—physically, mentally, and spiritually; and to make "meaningless
phrases" meaningful in the real business of living
together as a whole and wholesome organism.

3

This impulse is the foundation of "the great temple to come," to the building of which the war task has summoned the nation. It is to be evolved under a stress as difficult as the war itself and in the midst of the apparently conflicting and complex actualities of daily affairs. The war has laid the practical basis for the realization of this national faith by opening the way for a more vital unity in the whole life of the nation. The Revolution, the War of 1812, the Civil War, the Spanish-American War, each made its contribution toward a closer and larger federation of the units of the American State; but they were mainly steps in a territorial unity,—a superficial integration. The nation had not unified into its life the bone and sinew of its material life. The whole body of the activities by which its people lived and produced the wealth of the nation—its *business*, as the necessary product of science, invention, and work applied to the country's infinite resources as it grew in power and federated in larger units of power and service—instead of developing as a part of the nation's government, helped by it, and coöperating with it, was placed in the curious situation of being its enemy. It had within it the drive of reality that requires expression, and, in the full freedom it enjoyed, developed a power equal to that of the Government. The masterful men, whose creative genius for construction the great adventure of modern commerce and industry had developed, appeared somewhat paradoxically as the victims of an unpatriotic, self-centered materialism. The practical necessity of war mobilization has integrated business into the whole life of the nation, and in the simplest and most direct fashion revealed to it and to business itself its deeper relations to the life of the whole, and also its innately coöperative spirit. Its affairs are thus given a new and valid unity that will never be lost. Hundred thousand dollar men of business who work for the nation for one dollar a year will never again hold superfluous wealth in exclusive esteem; and business that gives itself in devotion to saving the nation for humanity will be far more open to humane ideals; the constructive genius that sought satisfaction in the productive organization of big business will not fail to get a fresh vision of the larger whole for which that organization exists, and by which its creation is made possible.

That this fuller unity precipitated by the war emergency has paved the way for a more effective mobilization of democracy in its steadily progressive effort to transmute "a society not yet humanized" into a society that wields its knowledge and its industrial power in behalf of a democratic culture, is the common thought of the nation. The new nationalism finds its faith in the fact that science has made a fresh interpretation of democracy possible through a new access of productive power that it has liberated, by relieving human labor, and vastly multiplied its results. Vital forces have found a new and inspiring expression, and will give current form to the eternal topic of civilization; the whole free man seeking a clear path to merit of whatever kind in the environment of his daily affairs.

It is to leadership in this world adventure of the nation that the American university is called,— not as an institutionalized formula, but as the mobile organism for interpreting the actual forces that constitute our present national life in terms of a freer and more complete humanism. This has always been the real university function. The ancient universities owed their origin to this deepest instinct, and wherever and whenever the university has been vital, it has been because it has been vividly conscious of that supreme function.

Jefferson with prophetic vision saw implicit in the new nation a new civilization, and for the realizing of that the need of a characteristic institution. He drew up the plan for a university that would not only embody in its curriculum the traditional culture values of Europe, but, as he said, "would harmonize and promote the interests of agriculture, manufacture, and commerce." The evolution of the American university has been the record of the fulfilling of Jefferson's foresight. It has paralleled the development of the nation.

To the older types that seek to express man's inner life and his relations to the past, it added those that express his outer life and his relation to the present. It seeks to reassert for present civilization what past civilization says to America, together with what America has to say for itself. Through its colleges of liberal arts, pure and applied science, professional and technical schools, it repeats the culture messages of the past century: Arnold's message of sweetness and light, Huxley's message of the spirit of inquiry, and Carlyle's message of the spirit of work. But in this grouping of the college of culture, the college of research, and the college of vocation into an organization of efficient and specialized parts it has remained compartmental. It has not sufficiently focused its whole purpose for its own students to be clearly conscious what it is, or indeed for them to be assured that it has one. And yet it is altogether clear that it cannot realize its present supreme opportunity and obligation of interpreting America until it mobilizes its own complete life.

This thought of a whole, unified purpose does not carry with it the criticism that the university has been too devoted to specialized abstractions, nor that there should not be a variety of interests within the whole. On the contrary, it takes for granted the infinite value of the development of pure science, for instance, and the fact that the life of modern learning depends absolutely upon it.

It does mean to give emphasis to the forgotten commonplace that the university as an intelligent purpose organism must know what, as a whole, it and the society of which it is a part are driving at; and as an American university that it must interpret as pointedly as possible the forces that stir the soul of the nation. Full acceptance for this or that study or group of studies depends on its interpreting them in spirit and method in terms of the university's deepest intent,—just as a business interprets one of its departments; and the university cannot exert its own full function unless it is able to digest and interpret the whole in terms of its whole conviction and insight.

The curriculum of the college—the medium for expressing its purpose—represents the historic effort of civilization to create a whole free man, and it might be expected that no student could go through the mill of it and escape getting a convincing picture of what that means as the present college sees it. But this ideal of the successful life is far less clear and less convincing to the average student (naturally docile, curious, and sympathetic as he is) after four years of college residence, than the ideal presented by business success in spite of its grotesque exaggerations. The severest judgment that can be made against an institution is that made several years ago by President Pritchett against the American college, when he described it as an organization where

success in the things for which it stands no longer
appeals to those within it. The difficulty is that
the whole thing for which it stands is no longer
clear to itself, in the radiant clearness of its focused
insight. For all of its brilliant achievements,
and its devoted individual service, it has not come
into the transforming conviction of its organic
mission of reconciling in creative works of art
and science and government the new idealism of
material America. That the message of the college and university appears to the student, not as
an interpretation of the whole life that he craves,
but as detached and somewhat eccentric postur-
ing, is due to the fact that its compartments are
short-circuited—the non-conducting mediums for
its larger ideas. Indeed the vital objectives of the
university are rarely if ever considered by the
group faculties, or by the faculty as a whole.
Occasionally in an opening address to freshmen
they get summary consideration when a faculty
representative defends or attacks the classics, or
the sciences, or the practical in education. The
fact that there appears to be any conflict is, and
has been in the past, due to the failure of the
universities to function as a whole organism of
interpretation as well as of specialized parts. The
difficult present situation of the classics in American education, for instance, is not, we may be
assured, because there is any less *use* for the
classics, nor because the value of the classics

themselves is discovered to be less for the practical
men of our period than it was for the men of fifty
years ago.   The difficulty will not be cured by
jeremiads against the age and vocational education,
nor by mere praise of the spirit of liberal learning
and its practical utility.   The difficulty is in the
organism of its interpretation.   Modern scientific
scholarship that, in many ways made possible a
new renaissance of the humanities, also actually
wrought them great harm.   Not as the direct result
of the victory of science in their historic battle for a
place in modern learning, but indirectly by "peaceful penetration."   Students do not get a whole
impression of the liberalizing effect of the message
and spirit of the humanities.   They are told that
it is there—and it *is* there, and as wonderfully
alive as ever; but it remains for the most part
unresurrected, because it is the victim of an institutionalized, desiccated technique.   The same
criticism may be made of other divisions of the
curriculum where academic inbreeding threatens
to crystallize the parts and institutionalize the
organism on which the healthful, robust life of the
university and that of the nation depend.

Culture as learning, science as investigation,
and work as utility, each has an eternal life of its
own, and to perfect each of them for the performance of its special work will always be an aim of
the university, each making its own value and
relation to the whole clear; but this conception

of its function as a university is necessarily partial and transitional. Tyndall, in his great Belfast address made in 1874, points out that it is not through science nor through literature that human nature is made whole, but through a fusion of both. Through its attempt to make a new fusion of both with work, during the great constructive years of the past half-century, our civilization has caught the impulse of a new culture center. It is this that the university must express. It is more than an aggregate of parts. As a university it is a living unity, an organism at the heart of the living democratic state, interpreting its life, not by parts, nor by a summary of parts, but wholly, —fusing the functions of brain and heart and hand under the power of the immortal spirit of democracy as it moves in present American life to the complete realization of what men really want. The real measure of its power will be whether, discarding the irrelevancies of the past and present, it can focus, fuse, and interpret their eternal verities and radiate them from a new organic center of culture. This it must do, as the heart of a nation endowed with a soul, and it must do it in terms of present American life, though not as the champion of a specific social program. It sees its problem as positive, not negative; as one of fundamental health, not of superficial disease. It looks on the state as a producer; not as a policeman. It is not so much concerned with doing a certain set of things, as infusing the way of doing all things with a certain ideal, as the intelligent culmination of an invincible human purpose. Not by spasmodic reform, nor by sentiment, nor by the expiations of philanthropy; but by understanding, criticism, research, and applied knowledge it would reveal the unity of the channels through which life flows, and minister to the purification of its currents. It would conceive the present state and all of its practical problems as the field of its service, but it would free the term from the narrowing construction of immediate practice. The whole function of education is to make straight and clear the way for the liberation of the spirit of men from the tyranny of place and time, not by running away from the world, but by mastering it.

In the immediate sense that the war is a conflict involving all the resources of the nation's present life, to be won through the absolute commitment of all of its massed forces now, or handed down as a burden of future generations, the sole question of the American university is the practical one of immediate victory. And in the larger sense that the war is merely a phase of the larger and even more heroic adventure of making real the aspirations of men to win full freedom in the realm of the creative spirit, the question is also a practical one. In that, the American university has the central and determining part.

In its courses and perhaps in its organization it will be influenced by the forces of practical education that, in the war emergency, have extensively entered its life. In pure and applied science its work will be vastly stimulated. But far more significant will be the inspiration of all the component ideas and ideals of its spiritual life as the representative interpreter of a nation to which has passed the spiritual leadership of western civilization. It is a task with opportunities and obligations beyond those that have hitherto fallen to any nation, and therefore to any nation's characteristic institution. It calls for qualities of independence, courage, vision, and for faith in its own original genius, and for the warm, robust sympathy of life on the open road—"with thought like an edge of steel and desire like a flame." It is an effort to liberate the ideal as a fighting force in the common affairs of men; and in these terms the American university will give effective answer to the nation's fateful question: "What in the way of clear guidance have you to offer, or must we look to another?"

PATRIOTISM AND THE SCHOOLS[1]

I CONFESS, my fellow teachers, that I very eagerly accepted the invitation of our President to speak to this Assembly, and the subsequent suggestion of our Secretary that I adapt my remarks to what is called a patriotic program. My theme is "Patriotism and the Schools," and as a teacher, I gladly seize the opportunity to talk with you briefly about what seems to me to be their startlingly significant present relation—not because I presume to have any strange new thing to say, nor eloquent way in which to say it; but rather because in the direct fashion of sincerity I am happy to try to interpret your own thoughts about the teacher's share in this supreme business that now absorbs the world.

President Wilson said the other day that "Service and sacrifice must come from every party, every creed, and every profession." As teachers we are ready to meet this issue, and to meet it with the knowledge that war is the fire test of every individual and every profession. Stripped of all

[1] An Address before the North Carolina Teachers' Assembly at Charlotte, N. C., November 30, 1917.

44

pretense and lip-service, we are ready to answer in stark honesty whether there is now any especial or essential service that we can render our country in the hour of its trial, and whether there is any valid sacrifice we may make that will let us face with eyes equal and unashamed the splendid youth who as soldiers give "the last full measure of devotion."

I am quite confident that as we meet here in this most critical year in our nation's history we mean to answer for our profession and for ourselves in terms of an exalted patriotism whose new standards of distinctive service and complete sacrifice will both justify and glorify our part in a struggle that can do no less than open a new volume in the history of mankind.

It is because this patriotic desire on the part of teachers is so clear, and because the nation's need and task stand ready for the shaping of our hands—and for no other hands than ours—that the present moment, far from being, as I heard a distinguished educator recently say, "The most disheartening moment in the history of education," is, on the contrary, and by all odds, the most inspiring. Any failure of teaching as a profession fully to justify itself in this supreme test will be due not to a lack of opportunity nor to a lack of essential patriotism. The life of the teacher in peace is perhaps more directly that of the patriot than that of any profession. Any failure will be due to just this attitude of sullen discouragement in the face of disaster—inability to readjust our profession of peace with the prophetic swiftness required by the exigencies of war, because the fire of our inspiration has been deadened through the monotony of our daily tasks and the glowing heart of it lost under the gray ashes of routine and indifference.

I heard a man say the other day—in a group talking about Red Cross, Y. M. C. A., and Liberty Bond campaigns—that he was glad the war had not really "come to" him. "I am a teacher," he said; "war is antagonistic to my profession.   Besides, I have enough trouble inside the schoolroom, without thinking of the gloomy things outside."

There is no "outside" in the world to-day; its destiny "is all in one bottom trusted." Three years ago this country thought in the terms of this teacher's remark.   Its temper and intent were those of a separate organism in the world of men, working out its destiny in peace apart, happy in the heritage of the free institutions it had transplanted from its European home, rich in the material bounties of Providence, busy with its difficult tasks, jealous of its own separate life.

Then came the thundering revelation of the great war—first as a thrilling spectacle, then as a growing terror from its proximity and merciless destruction; and then, in the lightning flashes of

its deeper insights, the true spiritual revelation
of its meaning—through the consciousness that
we, in the silent processes of the world's growth,
had been inextricably bound into the heart of the
destinies and brotherhood of the race.   Then followed our entry and consecration, whole and complete, to the righteous settlement of the world issue
of life and death so joined.

It is a life and death issue, on a scale of unimagin-
able destruction, from the point of view of practice
or ideals: for the world, and so for us as a nation,
as North Carolinians, as teachers, as individuals,
and for our children and our children's children.
This world for us is in no real sense the place it was
when this Assembly met twelve months ago.   It
had gathered all of its treasured resources of material, human and spiritual wealth, from generations
of construction, and staked them all on this single
hazard of what Bismarck called "God's iron dice."
Fifty-three million men have been enlisted—the
physically best of the human race; of these, twelve
million have been killed or permanently disabled
in the first three years—five times as many as in
the twenty years of the Napoleonic wars.   The
daily cost of this destruction is $160,000,000 and
military costs alone have crossed a hundred billion
dollars.   In addition, there is the unreckoned destruction of cities, railways, factories, bridges, roads;
and the loss of the millions of men who have been
withdrawn from ordinary industry.

It is not important further to recount these utterly unthinkable figures, nor to review the causes that made the sacrifice necessary. We teachers have a practical human interest there as trustees of the common property and life of the world, and as practical men and women we can interpret its significance and measure our interest in its result in the practical terms of Servia, Poland, Belgium, the *Lusitania*, Louvain, Edith Cavell, and what these and the other black pages in the record stand for.

As practical American men and women we can interpret it and measure our interest in it, as a free and prosperous people, whose wealth and power was and is in the lustful eye of the Pan-German empire as surely as are France and England.

More than this, as practical teachers we can interpret it and fix the mark of our interest in its result by the ruthless violation of every fine and precious thing for which our civilization stands, and that we as teachers teach, and that gives us all of our authority as teachers.

In that we are men and women, as well as teachers, we have a fundamental, almost primitive, interest in this fight without quarter to make the world a place where men and women may pursue the real business of living without an armed guard, where a nation's faith and a woman's honor shall not be wantonly violated, and where the white, sunny walls of the gardens of simple folk shall not be splotched red with the blood of little children.

When I think of all of this material and spiritual destruction I cannot escape the conviction that there is nothing of concern in the world to-day compared to the terrible necessity of winning this war.

This aspect of the world struggle, from the point of view of practical men and women of the world, is not all, nor is it after all our main or deepest concern as teachers. If the war were a detached or accidental horror, we might, even while throwing ourselves whole-heartedly into the difficult task of destroying the military and political power of Germany, still feel that it is the most disastrous calamity in the history of education and of the race—to be fought without regret indeed, and yet with small constructive recompense.

But far from being such a detached and unaccountable accident, this is its inspiring and even sublime compensation: that the time is at length ripe for the final settlement for the whole world of the conflict between two irreconcilable ideals governing the relations of men, that are at the roots of all human progress—a conflict toward which from a thousand detached battlefields the currents of history have been converging through all the patient centuries. From that early dawn of time when man made his first accidental fire captive (some solitary cave man—the isolated

4

enemy of all living things) and nurtured that fire in his fight against his fellow animals, and cold and hunger, to his latest conquest of space with the wireless, man's expanding and aspiring life has been a fight for just this ideal of freedom— to be freely at home, physically, mentally, spiritually, and politically, on this planet, and so master of his environment.

Through science and invention he steadily linked the physical world together and the political world, into wider and deeper units of understanding, and coöperation, and self-government; and the living spring that was the source of all his restless striving and suffering and sacrifice was the God-implanted, indomitable belief in his innate rights to life, liberty, and the free pursuit of happiness.

"Paganism utterly denied such rights. It allowed no value to a man as man; man was what wealth, or place, or power, made him. Even deep-visioned Aristotle, you remember, taught that nature intended some men to be slaves and chattels." It was the religion of Jesus Christ gathering up the wisdom of the struggling centuries that gave final status to man's value in the world of things in the proclamation of the common fatherhood of God and the brotherhood of man.

That means so infinitely much—this doctrine of men as the sons of God—in every human relation that we have not even yet caught its full significance. The history of the eighteen hundred years after Christ is the story of man's effort to understand and digest into practice that simplest and most wonderful of spiritual doctrines and apply it to the coöperative enterprise of living together that we call government. This practical attempt to put his civil and political institutions in accord with his spiritual faith came at last, and it came here in America. That is what America is. We said that by nature all men are free and equal, and that governments are of, by, and for all the people; that rights begin in and with the people and go upward from them, and not downward from the State. To the oppressed of all nations it meant a clear pathway to merit of whatever kind; it meant having an infinite chance and knowing you had it.

The shot that was fired at Concord as a proclamation of the divine right of the individual in government was heard around the world—in England, no less than in America and France. Following the French Revolution, and the mediæval despotism imposed on the states of Europe by the settlement of 1814–15, freedom made its separate fight in Italy, Austria, and Germany, and by 1848 there was the vision of "Europe as one great emancipated land." But that fabric of the dream of freedom collapsed, as it had done so often before, and under the leadership of Bismarck in

Germany absolutism became once more ascendant, to remain so for seventy years.

Bismarck, at that time, clearly stated the issue; it is the issue now and will be till the world is wholly free. He said: "The strife of principles which has shaken Europe is one in which no compromise is possible. They rest on opposite bases. The one draws its law from what is called the will of the people. The other rests on authority created by God"—by which he meant hereditary military despotism. And he stated the logical method of carrying out this policy: the method of "blood and iron." The issue is the same, the method is the same; the glorious difference is that instead of its being a conflict in separate states or federations, as it has always been before, and as Germany sought to make it in 1914—instead even of its being a fight to make merely Europe "an emancipated land," it is now a clear fight to a finish, and without quarter, between national self-government and military despotism, humanity and Germanity, for the liberty of the human race and the whole trend of international and civilized evolution.

And yet the success of the cause of freedom is not more certain now than it was for European freedom in 1848. Some time ago President Wilson spoke of Germany as "balked but not defeated." Since then her situation has become far better. She is now, in terms of military conquest, much nearer the realization of her dream of Pan-German Empire than she was three years ago. She has twenty-five million troops at her disposal and forty million slaves from partly conquered races providing food and munitions for her. She fights with weapons of her own choosing, with a war machine constructed by the coördinated power of science, industry, and education through forty years.

I believe, as you do—and as Mazzini said in 1849 in exile—in the ultimate supremacy of the forces of the free human spirit. If I did not I should have no faith in life at all. But democracy, though "a glorious thing to fight for, is a poor instrument to fight with. We are as aggressively organized for the extravagances of peace as Germany is for the extravagances of war." The certainty that we feel in our victory in this contest rests less on a reasonable analysis of the war situation than it does on our comfortable faith in our manifest destiny. But destiny takes no interest in *when* it does its work; it has no concern with time. It is not impelled to win freedom for the world in the twentieth century any more than for Europe in the nineteenth. *Destiny becomes manifest for democracy when it takes the form of popular constructive will and purpose.* The present fight will be won not by the organization of the Government in Washington, as swift and effective as that has been, but by the organization of the people behind the Government. It will be won not merely by the five or ten million men whom we organize and train to fight abroad; but also the ninety-five million who are organized to work, and save, and serve together at home.

Our Government has from the first realized the vital necessity of this unity in national effort, and for the need of raising it to the point of burning intensity (just as Germany feared it and spent millions trying to thwart it), and called into being many agencies to bring it to a focus. But no agency exists or can be created in this work of essential statesmanship comparable in power—and I say it not because I am talking to teachers, but because it is my deepest conviction—to that of the teachers and the schools. And this is true, both from the view of the immediate practical needs of civic preparedness—as necessary now as military preparedness was three years ago—and also from the view of making the results of the war count in terms of its democratic purpose.

Let me, then, as quickly as I can, put a definite point on our present American status in its relation to the schools and to us as teachers during the coming year.

A successful military decision for democracy depends now on America; and we may make that more definite by adding that the success or failure of American participation will be determined by what we do here in the next six months. This depends on whether we can reach the mind and

imagination of the people—the warm, wise, healthful heart of the folks back home—sympathetic,
but slow, hidden and wary, especially of anything
with a foreign smell to it. It is not a question of
whether eventually the imaginations of the people
will be lighted and their will fired; it is simply a
question of whether this certain condition can
be brought about by anything less terrible than
the privations of actual want and the heart-tearing
shock of the casualty list. To make the issue of
the war to end war more certain, to hasten its
end, if only by one day, we must get to every
American shop and street and fireside, in homely
understanding, the truth that the only economical,
horse-sensical, decent thing to do is *now* to put all
and every resource of our wealth, energy, brains,
and will into winning the war.

And when we say *all*, let us mean *all*, and judge
not by whether we have given much, but by
whether we have anything left. To get this done
we shall have to act and feel with a personal point
and passion that we do not now feel.

You may remember how all of the inhabitants
of the earth agreed on one occasion that at a given
signal they would give a mighty shout together
to reach the ear of the inhabitants of Mars. At
the given signal there was silence. Each man
decided to listen to the shout of the others. If
America reaches the ear of Mars we must act now,
as if the decision of the war depended not on

President Wilson's intelligence and insight, nor upon General Pershing's prowess and the 24-hour-a-day, 7-days-in-the-week devotion of his men, but to say in the inmost heart of us, and think and act the conviction: "*The issue of this war depends on me.*"

The fashion of a winning democracy, in peace or war, must be for each individual to act as a personal trustee of the result. So its leaders are the victorious incarnation of its spirit.

When I remind you that there are ten thousand schoolhouses, and fourteen thousand white teachers, distributed over the whole of North Carolina as spheres of influence covering the whole and the heart of its life, it is abundantly obvious that the teachers are the greatest possible potential power for meeting the nation's greatest present need. In order to respond to this opportunity on its simplest side, we need intelligently to read the newspapers, good weekly journals, and the Government publications, to master the facts of the war, not merely for their diverting stimulus as news, but as a capital concern of our own, and so be able to interpret them. We need to study and understand the reasons for and the fundamental importance of the food and fuel campaigns, and to be able to explain them so that the community will readily meet their increasing exactions. Our State Department of Education has just issued an admirable program for North Carolina Day

along this line of practical patriotism. This is
to be followed by four or five others in suc-
ceeding months for pressing home the thought of
community expression of the national spirit.

Our opportunity here is infinite, and should
take form in this concrete program of action: *Let
every teacher, man or woman, as a leader in his
community in every school in the State, from the
most elementary up through the colleges and university, so act as if the response of his community was
to be the response of the nation, and so the decision
of the world.*

But important as is this direct service in teaching the facts of the war situation and needs in
carrying out war plans, there is another less obvious and more vital relation. It is the fundamental effect that the war should have on
teaching itself; for in spite of the demoralizing
effect the war has had, and will increasingly have,
on school organization, the great fact remains that
its total effect ought vastly to ennoble and inspire
the whole profession of teaching through the new
responsibilities created. "In all ages," it has recently been said (President Alderman), "nations
sorely tested in war have turned from broken
adults to unbeaten youth for realization of their
hopes and dreams." Great revolutions, great
social changes, like the Reformation, the Renaissance, the French Revolution, are landmarks in
the history of education. Such an hour of almost

universal educational reconstruction has struck for us.

We teachers of North Carolina, in common with the teachers of the other states of the world, will, after this great war, to an extraordinary degree, have to meet this problem of the world's reconstruction, and also democracy's fundamental issue of whether the war is to be won by the winners.

Some of these problems immediately occur to you: (1) The problem of facing the world's tragic loss of men and loss of means. "The tragedy of the war," as Professor Fisher has said, "is not the destruction of wealth, lost art and treasures, or even the breaking of human hearts; but the injury to the fiber of human stock." (2) The problem of financial bankruptcy. Every nation is even now on a paper basis except our own. (3) The problem of demoralization of the world. Its ethical and other standards will be shaken and tested out as its financial organization has been. (4) The problem of making a free people efficient and competent in self-government is yet to be solved—to demonstrate that, given the right to choose freely, men will choose to live rightly. We are to form after this war, as men have after every great human upheaval, a new concept of what it means to be a good man and a good citizen.

All of these problems are problems of the teacher. They are to be determined partly by what happens to the millions of men in France under Pershing; but ultimately and absolutely by what happens to the millions of boys and girls whose plastic minds are now under you and me and the other teachers of the nation.

What is especially in point here is not that we should now turn our attention in the schools to the solution of these problems, and others that may suggest themselves, but that their certain oncoming brings to us that enriched and exalted interest in human life that is the source of all our productivity as teachers. The need of the world for the intelligent and sympathetic leadership that constitutes the distinctive service of teaching makes freshly luminous the great and joyous job we have to do in the world and gives to us a new inspiration for doing it superlatively well.

What the nation and the world seem to say to us here is: *that we should teach as if each boy and girl before us, whose life is entrusted to our shaping, is to be the boy or girl who is to do the reconstructive work of the thousands of the potential statesmen, scientists, poets, merchants, and artists who have been slain.*

When Mr. Wilson said that in making war on Germany America had no quarrel with the German people, he said a strange and wonderful thing to two nations at war, and a thing that aroused dissent almost as violent in America as in Germany. We have come to understand and accept the fact that though we are to give millions of

lives and sink billions of dollars in this struggle,
yet even in the event of complete victory we shall
ask not a dollar of compensation nor the extension of national authority over one foot of new
territory. Our victory is not in the old terms of
conquest nor in them is the source of our national
authority among men. Our nation and its authority are *just what its power to reflect and actualize the aspirations of men makes it.* Mr. Wilson
meant to say that if the Germans could come to
understand what America truly means they would
know that the war is for them, and for all men
everywhere quite as much as it is for us.

We have not, perhaps, sharply asked ourselves
what our full meaning is, nor have we come to
understand just what form the thought that now
deeply stirs the soul of the nation will take.
But the essence of our meaning is clear, and daily
it is becoming clearer, as the source of the nation's material and spiritual strength in this immediate crisis, and the guarantee of its benign
and wholesome reconstruction after the war.

It is just this simple fundamental that the world
gets and then forgets—of the supreme rights of
human life as such. We mean to give a new
importance to that, and to get new extensions and
applications of it in all our relations through a
more real and genuine sense of its divinity as
manifested by ourselves and all other men in all
our relations; and we mean to say, I think, that

no other concern is comparable to its nurture
and development, regardless of whether it touches
our business, our religion, our politics, or our education, or whether it concerns a cook, a factory
child, a farm hand, a clerk.   We mean to say, too,
that a human life has more value than the longest
column of figures in the world, and that the life
of a little child has more weight than the trade
balance of the nations.   This we are coming to
know as the meaning of America, and this is the
prophetic voice in which the new world will answer
in actualities the aspirations of the old.

"One knocked on the door, and a voice asked
from within, 'Who is there?' and he answered,
'It is I.'   Then the voice said, 'This house will not
hold me and Thee,' and the door was not opened.

"Then went he into the desert and fasted and
prayed, and returned again, and the voice asked,
'Who is there?' and he said, 'It is thyself,' and
the door was opened."

The world is unifying itself in this terrible ordeal
of fire to write, not for us alone, but for all mankind, a new chapter in progress in new terms of the
divine nature of human life, through which, under
God, we shall have a new birth of material and
spiritual freedom.   And of this, that is nothing
less than a new center of gravity for all human
conduct, the priest and prophet of democracy,
whether peaceful or militant, is the teacher in
the schools of the nation.

II

CULTURE AND CITIZENSHIP

CULTURE AND COMMERCIALISM[1]

"He turns a keen untrammeled face
Home, to the instant need of things."
KIPLING'S *An American*.

I

THE words that stand at the head of this essay
are, it is confessed, a little threadbare. They
have both been overtalked. Commercialism, to
be sure, has not had much to say for itself, but it
has been persistently talked about. It has been
abused for its unspirituality, for its vulgarity, for
its tyrannical dominance over American life. Its
antonym and antidote is understood to be culture.
In the common usage to which this word culture
is subjected it means the more or less superficial
refinement that is concerned with taste and knowledge. The identifying of commercialism with
vulgarity is of course unfair; and the convention-
alizing of culture into a matter of books and
knowledge is unfair, too, for it is a species of
narrowness with which real culture can have

[1] From the *South Atlantic Quarterly*, April, 1908.

nothing to do.   To distinguish it we may call it academic culture.

It is to this academic culture that commercial America as a nation seems to be deliberately opposed, and it is academic culture that the average man on the street is a little contemptuous of. Real culture is broader.   It is nothing more specific than harmonious development of the individual spirit.   Human development has never approached the stage where it appears quite harmonious and perfectly poised; it is rather development under the leadership of some dominant idea seeking perfect expression.   True culture may not be even a little contemned by any man. On the contrary pursuit of some phase of culture is a part of every man's life, and a culture standard is necessary to every nation that attains greatness—that is, that makes a contribution to the progress of the race.

Matthew Arnold, the English apostle of culture, spoke with insight and final charm of the true essence of culture.   He did not substitute superficial taste and knowledge for vital development of the spirit, but his emphasis did fall upon knowledge as the means of spiritual development.   The cant phrase is not unrelated to his definition of culture as "a study of perfection," "a coming to know the best that has been thought and felt in the world."   He explained that it was making right thinking prevail; but acquisition of knowledge, perfection through coming to know the past and its traditions, is the basis that he discovers. His program of making right thinking prevail was rejected as vague and impractical by his contemporaries, and his conception of culture appears after all as academic and limited.

That Arnold's critics were the stout representatives of the rising working class is not strange. A steady consideration of his scheme will show clearly that the working class are the supporters of it, rather than direct participants in it. Freedom from "work" is necessary to it. Leisure is what this cultivation makes precious; and work is inferentially vulgar and slavish. Academic culture implies a leisured class, it implies the classical idea that the perfection of the race is attained properly through the perfection of a specially nurtured group. The best atmosphere and conditions for this whole idea were found in Greek life, whence with modifications it has come down to us. The Greeks made specific limitations—curiously trivial some of them appear to us—on the activities of a cultured man. Plato and Aristotle declared that all work that requires physical strength is degrading, and Demosthenes in a popular oration taunts Æschines with the accusation that in his youth he was guilty of manual labor.

The European and English idea of culture was formed on the Greek concept. A few years ago a

violent newspaper discussion was aroused by the
fact that members of an American crew competing at Henley were protested because they had
worked their way over on a cattle-boat and therefore were not gentlemen.   There is no purpose to
over-emphasize the illustration; it is cited to
bring into relief the fact that the academic concept
of culture insists not merely that a man shall develop his spirit by studies and all gentlemanly
exercises, but that he shall not degrade himself
by manual labor.

The feeling that active labor is opposed to the
highest development is the basis of the unanimous
condemnation by foreigners of American civilization.   In a half dozen recent authoritative criticisms—English, Russian, French, and German—
there is agreement that life in America is merely
a race for wealth; that it is altogether vulgar;
that "the American does not remember, he does
not feel, he lives in a materialistic dream," . . .
for him "life has no beauty." Going back to
Arnold we come directly on the basis of this
criticism in his criticism of Cornell, one of America's most typical institutions of culture: "It is an
institution built on a misconception of what culture truly is and calculated to produce miners or
engineers or architects and not sweetness and
light." Arnold would admit that good miners
and good engineers and good architects are well
enough in their way, but culture is not interested

in the making of them; even in a way, they are illustrations of what culture is not.

Ezra Cornell founded the institution that bears his name because he felt that a true university is not merely a place where some fortunate few may come to know and to feel fine and beautiful things: his point of distinction was that it must also be a place where all men may learn to do well all things that need to be done. He must have felt that this business of knowing how to do is also culture, and needed institutional expression. Matthew Arnold looked at the effective product of this American workman and rejected it as false. If one compares Cornell, or Columbia, or the strong universities of the Western States, or better still the multiplying technical colleges—in glib American economy of nomenclature, "A. & M." colleges—if one will put these institutions in view with the convincing charms of Arnold's own Oxford, his criticism will appear but mildly to express the shock he must have felt. The contrast is indicative of the essential difference between the culture ideals of the life of which these institutions are the expression. The sum of the difference between the civilization of the Old World and that of the New may be stated thus: Work or business, or, as it appears, money-making is here an end in itself; abroad it is a means of buying leisure to travel, to study, in a word to cultivate oneself.

To state it so is to condemn it in the eyes of

many good Americans. They mistake the traditional European standard which served well its
time and place, for the completely universal
standard. The clear fact that the main current
of American life has been relentlessly set in another direction instead of leading them to despair
should suggest that it, too, is impelled by the
perfecting principle of a universal idea. Other
considerations thrust themselves forward. Leisure and caste, the basis of academic culture, is an
impossible basis for American life. So America,
generally speaking, has failed to make any but
weakly imitative or weirdly original contributions to conventional art or literature and but
slight contributions to conventional culture in any
form. Yet it has made important contributions
to the spiritual progress of the race. These have
their obvious origin not in leisure and caste, but
in the precisely opposite principles of Work and
Democracy.

II

Whether American life has substituted anything
for the old world standard that it abandoned is a
question which Americans at large have cared
very little about. The value of academic culture
has been kept steadily before the public eye; the
lack of it the average citizen acknowledges, however, with indifference—though not in the spirit

of vulgar self-satisfaction implied in the foreign
cartoons that conventionally picture Uncle Sam
as a hog. A great though more or less unconscious
idea of real culture is behind the undeviating
commercialism of the United States. Minor
manifestations of it are the establishment of institutions with the ideals that moved Ezra Cornell,
and the forcing of the colleges founded upon old-
world standards, and crystallized around the
classics, to conform in some degree their traditional curricula to the standard of American life.
Larger manifestations of this culture spirit evi-
dencing great vitality suggest as an answer to the
indictment that the persistent materialism of the
United States is opposed to the spiritual development of the individual and the race, that this
civilization is, on the contrary, the one great
progressive movement in present world development. Men will never again be satisfied quite
with the culture pursuits of Arnold—with measur-
ing lines from Keats and Wordsworth against
lines from Shakespeare and Homer. Cultivation
through the refinements of knowledge—the priceless sensitiveness to true beauty that leisurely
unfoldment brings—in its devotion to *being* loses
sight of *doing*, in its devotion to the subtle loses
sight of the obvious, in its pious reverence for the
past revolts against the necessary garishness of
the present.

In pointing out the moving force in contempo-

rary spiritual progress Tolstoy is nearer the truth
than Arnold. In *What Is Art?* he phrases the
fundamental culture motive thus: "In every period and in every society there exists an understanding of the meaning of life which represents
the highest level to which the men of that society
have attained—an understanding defining the
highest good at which that society aims. The
religious perception of our time, in its widest
application, is the consciousness that our well-
being, both material and spiritual, lies in the
growth of brotherhood among all men—in their
loving harmony one with another." All art, he
declares, is valued finally by its consonance with
this highest general aspiration of its time.

Here he defines an aspect of real culture and
finds its present field to be in the personal relations
of men.   His analysis, verified in essence by recent
world movements, recalls our attention to the
commonplace that life is larger than literature,
art, or science. Culture is the complete art of
life, and Democracy is its main active manifestation.

Along with the vague doctrine of Democracy,
groping its way through dark ages of repression
toward the present twilight, along with Democracy, came the principle of Work—active material
effort. To illustrate both, a stage for a billion
of men to live prosperously together on, an infinite
opportunity for the development of their construc-

tive faculties—an infinite *job*—was needed, and
America was discovered. Its whole subsequent
history has been an effort at perfection through
recognition of Democracy and Work as true ideals.

Work and achievement and not greed are the
basis of commercialism, just as the basis of a
sound Democracy is work; and work is in itself
a spiritual function and capable of developing
the spirit. It is an end just as much as it is a
means to an end. For this, typical Americans
are content to "die in the harness." The eleva-
tion of work to a place of dignity in this country
was not merely because of the necessity of conquering the country, and not because it was recognized as a basis of a sound Democracy, but
just because it satisfied a need of spirit.

. Recognition of the spiritual value of work came
as Democracy painfully emerged into practical
acceptance. It came, too, with the triumphs of
the nineteenth century in science quite as naturally as humanism followed the discovery of the
classics. Humanism emphasizes art, science emphasizes the dry light of fact, and work emphasizes
the application of fact to life. Humanism emphasizes feeling, science emphasizes knowledge, work
emphasizes will. So Arnold pled for a culture
primarily æsthetic, Huxley for a culture through
science, and Carlyle for a culture through work.

Carlyle gives this strong expression to what is
properly called his gospel of work: "Work is of a

religious nature . . . a brave nature, which is the aim of all religion to be. There is a perennial nobleness and sacredness in Work . . . in idleness alone is there perpetual despair. . . . Work is communication with Nature . . . the real desire to get Work done well itself leads more and more to truth, to Nature's appointments and regulations, which are truth. . . . An endless significance lies in Work, a man perfects himself by working." And as if this were not enough to say, he adds: "Destiny has no other way of cultivating us than by Work."

This is giving to the deed done well and the spirit of doing it recognition in the scheme of spiritual education. And there is spiritual uplift in every sort of material construction, in achievement, in consciousness of power to do. Emerson saw it when he said: "The purpose of culture is to train away all but pure power." So it is not by chance that this Yankee Plato, quite in contrast to the Greek philosopher, advocated some form of manual labor as necessary to culture. Nor is it altogether accidental that the great Philosopher, who transformed all of religion's dogmatic laws into Democracy's one cardinal principle, was Himself by profession a carpenter.

The general meaning is that the finest expression of the best self may be reached through the medium of effective right-spirited work. To say that culture in its broadest and most significant

sense may be realized through material achievement is as axiomatic as to say that progress toward
perfection may be made through sincere living.
Truth, we are told, is not in the words of seers,
but even in the lives of "one of the least of these
little ones"; and so culture, which is *truth alive*,
is not wholly in any words or things whatsoever,
but only and wholly in the fact of a sincerely and
profoundly lived life—a fact that our observation
of the perpetual round of business irritations, and
shortcomings makes us always likely to forget.

The culmination of work is material prosperity,
and commercialism is in essence nothing but the
scheme of life under which a race of successful
workers live. Steadily behind the social and artistic movements of history commerce has led a
life of its own. Its iron arms upheld the artistic
triumphs of Venice, of Holland, of Elizabethan
England; but the so-called material concept, the
concept of commercialism, never had full power
to express itself until the republic of America,
extended over an imperial continent and dowered
with infinite natural wealth, came into the conviction that work and not leisure was the symbol
of worth and the measure of equality.

III

In no particular has the American ideal so
strongly displayed its organic power as in subdu-

ing into unity the diverse elements that constitute its citizenship.   The Union, the political expression of the constructive ideal, is just now coming into real existence.   The culminating achievement of unification was the result not of a clash between geographical divisions of the country merely; it was a clash between culture ideals. The Union is a fact not merely because Lee surrendered to Grant, but because Lee's surrender was the first step in the surrender of a sectional belief in leisure and caste to the national ideal of Democracy and Work.   It was the vivid clearness with which Lincoln saw this ideal that gave to him his heroic greatness and inspired his belief in the Union with religious fervor.

The learning of the new ideal was to the South the great fight.   After the war the whole country became the battle ground of an absorbing economic struggle.   In the contest, pitiably handicapped, the task of the South was forced upon it. It was the titanic task of complete material reconstruction.   In the gloom of bitter oppression, while the untrammeled North and East, under the nurture of national business laws, were constructing great business enterprises, while the untrammeled West was turning a fertile wilderness into immediate wealth, the South was in the throes of a passionate struggle merely to exist.   Years followed years of grim, discouraging effort; but from this necessary work of reconstruction came the lessons of work, its dignity, its true worthiness, its rewards. Work became spirit and dwelt among us.

The simple resultant fact is that in the past few years the South has become prosperous. It has also become possessed of the exhilarated sense of prosperity. The fact does not remain superficial, however, for below it lies the fact that the South has yielded or is yielding to commercialism. National integration is the large resultant fact, and an immensely significant fact it is in present American history to the nation and to the section; because it is under the glow of a completely national spirit that "a nation becomes most intelligent, alive, and creative."

The South, then, presents the interesting picture of a nation that abruptly changed its culture source. An examination of what the South was before the Civil War and in its poverty afterwards, and what it is now, strikingly suggests the contributions of commercialism to the life of a people.

1. The South has come into the possession of a sound general basis for living. Up to the period of its commercial success it was chafing under the stress of material timidity and restraint. The mood of the South was precisely the mood that in individuals we call worry, and worry means productive paralysis, it means loss of all effective power. Poverty naturally produced introspection, sectional sensitiveness, and other phases of pro-

vincialism.   There was necessarily a lack of hope
in the future, a lack of confidence in the face
of great social problems.   The forceful success of
business enterprise changed all this.   It found a
sound physical basis for life.   The mood of worry
has been swept aside by buoyancy and faith; the
sensitiveness of a fearsome provincialism has given
place to a national consciousness that with widening trade relations will become international.
Liberation from the vassalage to poverty has
brought more than anything else spiritual liberation.   The very aspect of the streets of the towns
makes clear the fact that life is aglow with sound
material prosperity.   Ben Ezra strikes the note
of it:

> All good things
> Are ours, nor soul helps flesh more,
> Now than flesh helps soul.

2.   Added to this as a certain result of easing
the physical load of poverty we come on another
consequence of commercial success: it has brought
the South a larger point of view.   The subsiding
of prejudice and emotionalism in Southern life
is due in large part to business activity and business ideals.   Business has a temperamental opposition to violent feeling in all of its forms.   The
dollar is the one national symbol without sentiment or prejudice.   Commerce denies itself the
fine luxury of prejudice.   It knows no inheritance

of small feeling. Its relations defy local and personal limitations. Limitations that prevailed in religious, social, and political affairs are rapidly disappearing; women compete in every variety of business without prejudice to their social position; the force of ancestry is greatly diminished —a college student who waits on a table may be elected chief marshal of his class; the rallying cries of blind partisanship have less and less force —a politician who openly expressed a determination to vote for a Republican president was recently elected mayor of a solidly Democratic town. The logical end of the dominance of commercialism is the disappearance of the political unity known as the Solid South. Commerce is the one successful foe to party allegiance everywhere. It is even in temper, cosmopolitan in ambition, and the humanizing quality of tolerance follows always in the wake of trade.

3. In addition to these qualities of liberation commercialism has brought certain positive qualities. The activity of commercial endeavor demands a strong intellectual grasp on the forces of life. The qualities that come with this may be observed as the especial and distinguishing mark of present effective Southerners—the generation that is successfully expending its energies upon the construction of its immediate civilization. "Nicholas Worth," in his recently published autobiography, analyzes the Southern mood as oratorical, a vague

longing after nothing in particular. This record is a reminiscence of twenty or more years ago. Mr. Henry James, in his recent picture of Richmond and Charleston, visualizes the South as a figure somewhat blighted and stricken, seated in an invalid chair with a look of self-pity on its wrinkled face. The South Mr. James expected to find has to the romantic sense become that— a shadow of what memory still fondly dwells upon; but by her side Mr. James, in his concentration on the fading figure, failed to see the lithe, clear-eyed youth of tense muscle and heaving breast that his picture by contrast serves admirably to emphasize. What the immediate South is not, he shows us. Definiteness, accuracy, courage for details, quickness, confidence, power to organize, the strong ability to utilize the opportunities for effective living, these qualities of mind and character no less than of business, and formed in the stream of life rather than in pleasurable leisure, are qualities that the spirit that has lately come into its life has so emphasized as to make them appear new. That it has multiplied wealth may be said after all to be incidental, when placed along with the fact that it has given the South a great business class of social and intellectual efficiency that puts it in the front rank of the best forces of progress.

These are some of the characteristics of present and coming Southerners that have been acquired through the transference of the culture ideal. Although many beautiful things have no doubt been lost, what has clearly been gained is the inspiration of a great national spirit, the inspiration of equal opportunity through the physical well-being of all the people, freedom, tolerance, and intellectual grasp—qualities that make the modern American the world's most effective citizen.

The foundation of Southern effort that is now identified with commercialism is not the mammon spirit, the mere acquisition of money. It is the finer breath of an heroic effort to reconstruct a commonwealth that was wrecked. It is passion for building, building with the divine innate joy of a child, with the unalloyed enthusiasm of a man. It is the constructive spirit, and the idea that is ruling present Southern life is what for the want of a better word may be called the constructive idea.

No fact in present Southern life is clearer than that it is a beneficent passion. Not long ago a distinguished judge of the Supreme Court in a Southern State said to me with the simplicity of conviction: "If I had my life to live over I'd be an architect, or a contractor. I want to *make* something!" Making something is the key of the harmony. It runs through all gradations of achievement small and great, vitalizing every outlook upon life, every profession,—the vigorat-

6

ing idea of construction as opposed to analysis, criticism, retrospection, the backward look of regret. Behind the obvious facts of prosperity, materialism, commercialism, is the energizing, thrilling impulse, greatly and nobly to construct.

IV

In the nation at large the cultural results of commercialism are obvious in national characteristics and in the considerable contributions that the United States has made to the progress of civilization. A great English publicist recently said that five hundred years of world history would be made in the United States in the present century. He meant, it may be fair to interpret, that the free spirit of material activity would here quicken the heart and spirits of men into a deeper and truer adjustment of the relations of practical life.

That commercialism is altogether beneficent in its tendencies is most emphatically not suggested. It contains seeds of decay, as does every triumphant idea. Immediate history makes clear the fact that in the accumulated impetus of its effort it has overshot itself; but immediate history makes no less clear the fact that it has conserved power to correct its evils.

The corrective is the idea of Democracy. Democracy recognizes that power without service is

spiritual ruin.   The result of the recent upheavals
in business, and consequent revelations of business rottenness—if beginnings of reform may be
called a result—has not been a reaction in favor
of academic culture, nor has academic culture
been potent in effecting them.   It has been an
ethical reaction to bring back commercialism to
its rational moorings of Work and its business of
perfecting Democracy.

The contributions that America has made to
civilization bear consistent testimony to the belief that Democracy and Work are the heart of
its civilization and that they constitute a truly
cultural principle.   These contributions have not
been merely in the application of knowledge to
improved living through invention, although it is
significant that the United States furnished more
than one half of all the great inventions of the
nineteenth century; they have also been in the
application of fine feeling to life in carrying out
the principles of a sincere and efficient Democracy.
Achievement has been spiritualized by enthusiasm
for social betterment.

The following summary, made by President
Charles W. Eliot, of American contributions to
world progress, may be said to illustrate unexcep-
tionally this view: "(1) We have done more to
advance peacemaking than any other nation;
(2) We have set the broadest example of religious
toleration; (3) We have made evident the wisdom

of universal manhood suffrage; (4) By welcoming new-comers from all parts of the earth we have proved that men of a great variety of races are fit for political freedom; (5) We have diffused material well being among a whole population to an extent without parallel."

As we reflect upon these expressions of national life it is their spirit of service that denies them the category of crass materialism. The nation has shown under commercialism a capacity for fine feeling, and what is more, its main intent of making fine feeling prevail.

One of the most notable of recent national activities has been the policy of so-called imperialism. Critics at home and abroad have conceived this as but one more form of acquisitiveness and greed, tempting the nation to abandon its fine old doctrine of not meddling in foreign affairs. Such a view is superficial. What it lost was a selfishly safe isolation. Its policy of timidly conserving its own welfare became intolerable as its conquering commerce became international in scope, and it took upon itself the solemn function, full of dangers, responsibility, and reward, of a peacefully militant Democracy. The spirit of Democracy cannot remain inactive. It is made triumphant through commerce and it is consecrated by service.

The extensive compelling powers of the commercial idea in America Emerson saw with characteristic insight sixty years ago. "The development of our American internal resources," he said, "and the extension to the utmost of the commercial system, and the appearance of new moral causes are giving an aspect of greatness to the future which the imagination fears to open . . . the uprise of the new and anti-feudal powers of Commerce is the political fact of most significance at this hour." So it remains and will remain. It is the life fact of most significance. Then what shall be said of the aspect of greatness which this anti-feudal power holds in promise to present America with its wealth extended beyond Emerson's possible conception, throbbing with yet more complicated moral causes and unprecedented social problems? And this is just the beginning!

America has a culture standard by which in the long level struggle of time she shall be justified. The culture of a people is in the heart of the life that it lives and not in what by some past standard, however beautiful, it ought to be. To achieve a fully and harmoniously developed life for the individual and for the State is the only demand of culture. That typical men of America are not harmoniously developed is a criticism of life and not of commercialism only. Neither were the Chosen People of the Divine State, nor the Greeks under Pericles, nor the Knights of Arthur's Round Table harmoniously developed. Culture is not a knowledge of the creeds of religion, art, science, or literature. As American civilization confidently follows it, and it does follow it, it is not a study of perfection through "coming to know"; it is the development of the spirit through work—it is *achievement touched by fine feeling*.

v

Such is the general nature of the life movement in American civilization. Its motive force is an aspect of culture, not its adversary. In spite of its appearance of heedless, relentless development it asks for guidance and needs guidance. At heart American commercialism is spiritual and it will find its spiritual leaders and ministers. In making for new ports, old pilots are not altogether authoritative; but compasses are not abandoned, and pilots there will always be.

Where will American life find its true leadership, and what qualities will it insist upon in its spiritual leaders? One thing may be premised: they will not be Jeremiahs lamenting the lost gods of another civilization. They will know the sweetness and beauty of the past, but their main source of inspiration must be sympathy and identity with the strength of the present. They will deal with a present that emphasizes sweetness less than light; but a present that none the less is following truth and beauty. The professed

ministry of culture should make no mistake.   It
may learn from its own documents that the Gleam
has no eternal locus.

That educational institutions, the conventional
homes of culture, should revere the past, that
they should retain in their form of government
and curricula petrified splinters of medievalism
is natural; but in searching the past for things
that men have found good it would be unfortunate
if they should allow their eyes to become twisted
toward retrospection, if they should thereby neglect the fine task of making better the things
that men now find good.   The true apostles of
culture cannot be slaves to tradition; they must
be first of all sympathetic students of the present.
For them to be of real effect—for the terms "academic," "professor," "preacher," "literary," even
"cultured" ever to be other than marks of disin-
terested ineffectiveness—they must seize upon
the central idea of life with which they deal, work
with its spirit and supply its needs.

Before me lie two recent utterances from American colleges expressing dissatisfaction with the
work that is being done by these professional
leaders of culture.   One is a speech by a great
college president, who declares that the colleges
are not teaching effectively the things they pro-
fess to teach.   The other a speech by a brilliant
psychologist, who wonders if the conclusion of all
the boasted triumphs of educational institution-

alism will not be that the historian of the twentieth century will say that in this century colleges surrendered all real leadership to the "ten-cent magazines." Along with these there are others calling to the colleges to bridge the gap between traditional ideals and the needs of the people. All of them come from the colleges, indicating that there is in American colleges a pleasing contrast to the usual refuged cry of lamentation at the innate vulgarity of the people. The two points of view, of sympathy and revolt, constitute the problem, and to an extent one has to choose between them. If the apostle of culture finds that his principles allow him no sympathy with commercialism, the devotee of commercialism finds that his principles allow him no sympathy with that sort of culture. There is perfect equality in their contemptuous dissidence. Arnold saw with horror a wave break over England of "American vulgarity, moral, intellectual, and social"; he visited America, was cordially welcomed, was listened to with eagerness, and finally labeled by the keenly critical "reporters" as "an elderly bird pecking at grapes on a trellis."

In reviewing present conditions one ought to feel emphatically that the source of a large part of the vital strength of the country is in those professions of spiritual leadership, the ministry and teaching. The feeling is not strong enough to save uneasy doubt. A man or two, here and

there, stands out, but the feeling prevails that for
the rest they are distinctly and contentedly unim-
pressive, and as unrelated to the immediate life
problems of the mass of the people, retrogressive
in attitude and positively unthoughtful. The culture pulpit, as it actually exists for the average
man and the something more than average man
who constitute the American commonwealth, appears to be the daily press and some weekly
and monthly publications that with a certain
self-consciousness of their mission call themselves
"national."

For several years the church in America has
expressed its almost consternation at its loss of
the interest of the people, the loss of its ministers
of intellectual leadership. Professors in colleges
may not speak out on any subject of vital popular
concern and expect more serious attention than
such as hesitates between condescension and de-
rision. Very deeply branded into my mind as
fairly typical of the American attitude toward
these professions was a meeting I once witnessed
between a sensitive college professor and a prom-
inent statesman. The statesman extended two
fingers of his left hand to be grasped by the col-
legian, as he hailed with distinguished welcome
one whom the professor with some contempt
referred to afterwards as "a successful person."
The difficulty is not so much, it should be insisted,
that the business of professed culture leaders is

with the past, as that they have let it throw them
out of sympathy with the necessary business of
the present. If they have no part in the active
life of the nation, they have not altogether re-
gretted it. They may have deplored the popular
ideals, but they have not sought to find the heart
of good in those ideals and actively to make them
into something better; but rather they have
prized the seclusion into which the swift current
of national life has carelessly let them drift.

It is not strange that leadership should find
its perfect summary in the "untutored idealism"
of President Roosevelt; just as the constructive
spirit of the country does in the strenuous confusion of his multifarious activity. Whoever would
discover the spirit of America at the beginning of
the twentieth century will find the quickest way
to it through the biography of Theodore Roosevelt.
He approaches in the mind of the people the
heroic because he is the exhalation of their national life. It is here he touches the national
spirit, the national imagination. So all leadership must be from the standpoint of understanding
and sympathy. And leadership is what commercialism has the right to expect of education, of
professional culture in whatever form.

What Arnold's nonconformist critics said sar-
castically has some point in fact: "The Almighty
has a well-known preference for university men."
Knowledge is not resented, it is valued more than

ever; but to assume leadership it must always be applied to present life.   That is what commercialism and Democracy insist upon.

To attain this leadership positive qualities of activity and force are demanded of culture if it is to fulfill its real mission in the overwhelming tide of our successful life. It must display qualities of masculinity, of visible civic efficiency that wins a place as an equal rather than claims a sheltered corner as a traditional right and has it granted with the condescension that is bestowed on worthy weakness. Professional culture cannot afford to adopt the attitude of the poor relation to commercialism; the one always a mendicant who timidly keeps his place; the other a parvenu who brutally keeps out of his. American civilization will never make its best progress until a more organic sympathy is established between the two.

The source of American culture is American life. Professional culture must demonstrate its ability to foster and sustain vigorous life, courageously to lead strong men in the activities of sweetness and light, to carry on with energy the rough work of the spirit.

Sweet reasonableness is always the mood of culture, but sweet reasonableness is most admirable when actively displayed in time of stress. It must not be confounded with cloistered monasticism, academic immunity from discomfort, the selfishness that is no less characteristic of it than acquisitiveness is of commercialism. Let it become at all points, without reserve, to the full extent of its powers, the virile and militant citizenship of constructive culture.

Professor William James offers this suggestive warning: "If a college, through the inferior human influences that have grown regnant there, fails to catch the robuster tone, its failure is colossal, for its social function stops, Democracy gives it a wide berth, and turns toward it a deaf ear."

Conditions in this yet young Republic, with all its crudeness and aspiration, its innately splendid virtues as well as its vulgarities, cannot have less than the thrill of a challenge to formal culture, in as far as it is sincere, to do a man's part in the eternally new business of making a civilization.

PROSPERITY AND PATRIOTISM[1]

No perfunctory word of thanks can express to the membership of this Society my gratitude for the honor that your generosity has conferred upon me during the past year. To serve a society dedicated to the mission of patriotism, and confirmed in that mission by ten years of patriotic achievement, is an honor that no pretense of self-confidence will let me enjoy without misgiving. My gratitude is sincere, though I confess that it is somewhat ashamed.

It is my purpose to-night to speak on "Prosperity and Patriotism." In what I shall say I shall call your attention to the prosperous North Carolina of to-day, and our patriotic relation to it; and if my voice lacks the authority adequately to answer the simple but tremendous question I propose, I shall accomplish my purpose if I can put the question into your minds; for the relation between prosperity and patriotism must, in our present situation, be our preëminent concern.

[1] Presidential Address before the North Carolina State Literary and Historical Association at Raleigh, N. C., November 27, 1911.

And if it be thought that to avoid the obvious difficulties of looking at present things as they are, I mean to devote myself to criticizing things that I do not like, I hasten to correct that impression. Looking at North Carolina as she is I find my heart set to-night to a different tune. Too many genuinely good things invite judgment, too many that inspire hope and confidence to the very furthest reaches of patriotic faith, to suggest either vainglorious boasting or destructive criticism. Whatever is wrong in the complex problems with which we are so fortunate as to be confronted, and whoever is wrong on the questions on what North Carolinians are so fortunate as to differ, this much is squarely and fairly true: that the present moment in our State life carries more inspiration for the active enjoyment of constructive citizenship than any that the State has known before.

The main reason for this feeling of stimulation is clear. We have fought life's great necessary battle—the battle to make a decent and prosperous living—and we have won. There are plenty of economic difficulties still to overcome, but the sense of fear and worry is gone, the weariness is gone, the load has fallen from our back; and the average North Carolinian of to-day with straight shoulders and keen eyes looks at the world unafraid, confident that he can win material success to the limit of his ambition right here at home. And a tremendous thing that is to feel.

In spite of nine cent cotton and financial doubt
in the country at large, the news has been heralded
abroad that North Carolina is coming into a
magnificent legacy of material prosperity, and
men in joy and confidence are writing over the
rugged face of the State the epic of successful
work.

But in a more vital way than this constructive
materialism has North Carolina achieved success
that has brought civic stimulus and elation.
Along with this individual success she has in the
past ten years somewhat achieved the idea of community success through coöperation. Scarcely
a town in the State has failed to have its community spirit take fire from its constructive
materialism: town slogans, electric "Welcomes,"
chambers of commerce, civic committees of every
sort give evidence that prosperity has developed
the joyful sense of coöperative patriotism. In
the State at large prosperity has patriotically
achieved not only the public school system, but
the department of health and hygiene, of public
roads, historical and library commissions, and
numerous civic and betterment associations. It
has developed for this effort to make the State a
healthy and habitable home, its most competent
leadership: aggressive, efficient, almost inspired
by just the power of this thought of constructive
communityism.

Is this as far as we can go, or has patriotism a

profounder work to do, other lines on which to
work, other leaders to develop in a time of prosperous peace? In 1861 patriotism was exalted
by the supreme sacrifice of every physical thing;
in 1870 it was exalted by sacrifice not less supreme
and courageous. What is its mission in North
Carolina in 1911 when men are making money,
and the happiness of citizens is not greatly inter-
fered with by fighting for anything except success
in business? Domestic tranquillity is assured,
there is no need of the common defense. Can
a man have a prosperous business on Fayetteville
Street and still have a mission of progressively
achieving, and with high devotion, all of those
blessings of liberty for which his fathers gave "the
last full measure of devotion"?

Here we meet the oldest of personal and national problems: Can we translate prosperity into greatly permanent terms? To digest material
prosperity, government of the people confronts
a problem as difficult as the problem of science
when confronted with gravitation, Judaism when
confronted with Christ, monarchy when confronted
with America.

Moralists advise us to avoid this threat of
prosperity by despising money; culture tells us
to seek freedom of the spirit by despising work.
But we go on working; we go on making money.
We somehow doubt the efficacy of seeking perfection on an empty stomach. We are impelled

forward not because we do not want perfection,
but because as a free and equal people we seek
perfection through work, as surely as the Hebrews
sought it through religion, the Romans through
law, the Greeks through art.

Clearly we are going on, making as good a living
as we can, building great businesses and great cities,
achieving material success in terms that the world
has not known before.   I cannot hope to suggest
what I conceive this statement to mean for our
State.   We have scarcely begun this great com-
monwealth-construction.   America, we are told,
will one day be the home of 800,000,000 people.
Consider in these terms this North Carolina of
the future now in the making!   Will it be able
to assimilate its gigantic share of this regal wealth
of successful workers?   Will our civilization per-
petuate its buoyancy, its confidence, its progress,
or will it, like China, eat out its life and heart of
hope?   Right now we are facing great problems
of taxation, of race, of corporate control, of city
government.   What magnitude these will assume
the present conflict in the nation between government and business merely suggests.

The mission of patriotism was never higher,
its opportunity never more magnificent, than in
this formative period of prosperity.   Its ultimate
test is its ability to develop the whole life of the
people as individuals—whether the business man
on Fayetteville Street is to be merely a business

7

man, or Man-in-Business. The justice, benefi-
cence, beauty, and success of North Carolina depend ultimately and altogether on the presence
of these qualities in the life of the individual
North Carolinian. To master this constructive
materialism, to translate this prosperity becoming more and more triumphant, patriotism urges
every citizen to consecrate himself to achieving
as a part of his constructive civic program a
constructive idealism.

From the point of view, then, of this formative
prosperity, patriotism means above all things else
a profoundly genuine faith. It means faith in
these things we are doing as fine and worthy
things; it means faith in ourselves who are doing
them; it means faith in the race of men, and our
ability to incorporate into our lives the principles
that have made for their progress.

The Apostle Paul, who knew the life of money-
changing Jerusalem as well as that of Athens,
marks the supreme need in the daily work of a
free people when he says: "That was first which
is natural, and afterward that which is spiritual."
He suggests no apology for the industrial structure
of our prosperity, but he insists on its balance,
on its ideal interstructure. It is just with this
present business of ours that we have to deal,
not to discard it as unworthy, but to translate it
into worthy life. Patriotism urges us to have
faith in it; to have faith in the men who are

concerned in making it; the motives and capacities of our fellow North Carolinians, the active stuff of life that we have on hand—our contemporaries in the factories, on the farms, in the market place. Patriotism urges us to take abounding inspiration from a faithful view of the possibilities of progress in the activities in which we are engaged. It emphasizes not our competitions and dissensions, but our unities, reminding us that we grow on our appreciations, our admirations, our affections. A patriotic voice of sincerity and sympathy can, through civic faith, translate the life of any town, however mean and sordid, from impotence into power.

And so in State life. In organizing an admirable social life here, threatened as we are by personal ambitions, jealousies, party antagonisms, slowly dissolving poverty and its prejudices, and material success and its prejudices, patriotism urges us to submit ourselves joyfully to the works of unity, to the challenges to devotion, to the energizing virtues and ideals that are even more truly North Carolina's: her ideal home, her unrivaled stock, her noble traditions.

Patriotism makes potent in dealing with the garish problems of to-day the ideals of her past: the thought not only that her blood and spirit made great a nation across the sea, but that her blood had the hardihood to leave the nation, and as "a community so humble that no statesman condescended to notice it, reduced the wildest theories of civilization to practice"; and in addition to this vision of truth, caught a vision of righteousness by which that government steadily progressed; and in addition to this caught a vision of sacrifice by which in a war of exalted heroism she left immortal testimony of her bravery on every battlefield. Patriotism finds in these memories of her days of trial faith that she can as highly interpret the conditions of her present prosperity.

But patriotism in a prosperous State goes further than faith in its own activities, in its own contemporaries, and in its own history: it has faith in the race of men as capable of further and continued progress toward perfection. It catches a temper of loyal inspiration for its present effort, from its knowledge of what other nations have found good, in the ability of the people to know the permanently good and to choose it. It, therefore, has faith not only in what the men of to-day find good, but where that is short of completeness it would balance it and glorify it by unifying it with permanent standards. Wherever men have achieved fair memorials of progress, in whatever time or field or country, patriotism would find and follow and diffuse the principles of that progress. And in its review of history, the successes and bankruptcies of prosperity, patriotism finds no confusion. There is everywhere the same clear, simple judgment of history. I give it in the commonplace sentence of Bolingbroke: "Patriotism must be founded on great principles and virtues in the life of the people." Otherwise it becomes dead formalism. Religion forgets God and becomes Pharisaism and the letter of the law; democracy and prosperous commerce forget the people and depend on the machinery of legislation; identify progress with population, waterpowers, railways, skyscrapers, the opening of canals. These do not make a State great nor make men greatly love their State. "They are powerless until they give themselves to the reinforcement of those human qualities of which any real State life is made, and make the nation more just, more upright, more generous, more free, more love-inspiring. They may do that. It is within the power of a nation as of a man to grow greater with every dollar added to its wealth; but a dollar is powerless" until it joins itself to whole principles of life and passes into character. The character of a free people must assimilate its prosperity, as it forms, into the life of the people. And this is ultimately and simply what patriotism is in the life of a prosperous State: it is giving a welcome in the State life to all of those things, material and spiritual, which have the right to enter into it and dominate it.

As to what these principles are there is again no confusion. They have the simplicity and grandeur of all elemental truth. Paul, the apostle

of the people, calls them, "Whatsoever things are
true, whatsoever things are elevated, whatsoever
things are amiable, whatsoever things are of good
report," counseling us to let our lives run upon
their lines.   Plato makes the same judgment, more
comprehensively, as truth, goodness, and beauty.
Pasteur, the greatest of modern scientists and the
good patriot of progress, stated them in his final
message to mankind: "Happy is that man who
finds in his heart an ideal of beauty and obeys it,
an ideal of knowledge, an ideal of art, an ideal of
his native country.   These are the vital sources of
great thoughts and great actions."

To interpret the life of a people engaged in
triumphant materialism in terms of these ideal
values is the tremendous obligation of patriotism
in a time of prosperous peace: to incorporate
them in our lives, to project them into our affairs,
to make them supreme in our judgments.   It is
to give electric welcomes to these necessities of
the spirit that patriotism counsels us at this critical
moment in our history.   We need a baptism of
this patriotic faith—not a sprinkling, but an im-
mersion!   We do not need to change the spiritual
nature of North Carolina; but we do need to raise
its temperature to a temperature of power.   We
need to put the State more fully into that current
of spiritual power that runs through the humanity
of men as truly as the Divinity of God rules above
them.   All experience, all prophecy, and the high

instincts of our own hearts tell us that through patriotic faith and consecrated service we may translate our local issues in the terms of these eternal principles, and that only so shall our civilization see salvation.

Many sincere and patriotically disposed men grant that progress means more than material prosperity, but they will give to any program of idealism indifferent support because they regard it as too impractical for personal service.

They have the feeling that if we seek prosperity with heart, mind, and soul that the other will be added as a sort of extra dividend.   It is the always defeated hope of spiritual inertia.   If constructive idealism is to be the saving standard of our State life we shall establish it by effort, deliberate, courageous, and devoted.   The destiny of a people in ideals is no more a matter of chance than business is a matter of chance.   A certain fine basis exists in the nature of our people, but a high civic standard is not waited for, but achieved.

Others, more active, doubt the need of such a program for city or State because they identify progress of the people with party platforms.   In the midst of active affairs we are overwhelmed by the notion that democracy is a way of doing something, whereas it is primarily a good way of being something.   All of the active devices of government—ballots, laws, constitutions, and the rest—are not to enable men to vote, but to develop men who will vote for right things; not to make more perfect machinery for governing men, but to make more perfect men for governing. We can pass all the Sherman laws we please, but we cannot get them obeyed, enforced, or interpreted unless they accord with the vital standards and demands in the life of the people. There the issues of government are determined. That is what carrying the government back to the people really means; there is the true referendum. What most of us mean by faith in the people is a faith with limitations; a negative faith that they are not bad, that in a great crisis of right and wrong they will by a sort of instinct approximate right. We have not the high-hearted faith of the true democracy that sees in the developing ideals of the people the one fruitful source of a State's steadily progressing toward perfection. We believe in the average man; but we believe too much in his averageness, too little in his manhood.

There is another closely associated doubt as to the right of idealism to a place on a patriotic program: that it is indefinite and visionary, and so against the trend of the time. The trend of the time is toward practical efficiency, to identify education with useful facts, religion with works, and statesmanship with a tariff on mica. True patriotism does not rebel against this program except to say that it is incomplete. Patriotism is truly devoted to vocational training, to "swat-

ting the fly," to guarding the needs of the district;
but not as supreme ends in themselves. It looks
behind practice and immediate profit. It sees
that above all else the real fruitfulness of practice
comes from the supremacy of principles in the
lives of the people, and it has faith that its own
people are worthy of what the greatest nations in
their great moments have found as the inspiration
of their great achievements. In other words, it
rejects the standard of mere success that would
reproduce the very successful Pittsburg; the
standard of mere efficiency that would reproduce
the very efficient C. F. Murphy. But while it
values whatsoever things are true, and good, and
beautiful for their own sake, it does not leave them
an inactive philosophy. It does not reject practice, nor small affairs, but it saturates all practice
with ideal values and so makes it permanent and
magnificent. In every activity it is not ashamed
to insist that the standard shall be not merely
"Does it pay?" but that to that be added, not as
a dead echo, but as the supreme ultimatum of all
practice: "What doth it profit" if a State gain
the whole world and lose its hold on the realities
of Statehood?

The program of constructive idealism is difficult,
it is tremendous, but it is not indefinite. Above
and beyond all temporary considerations of property, railroads, factories, and corporations, patriotism lays hold upon its vision of North Carolina

as a noble state of mind and heart and soul, as
the Athens of Pericles was a state of mind, the
England of Elizabeth, and the Virginia of Jefferson. No tyranny of balance sheets can shake
the faith of patriotism in the great vital truth of
democracy that "without vision the people perish."

To catch this vision and to realize it is not the
patriotic work of any profession or class. All professions and businesses, all offices truly magnified, are equally the ministers of this patriotism
in a free and prosperous State. But it is the
singularly fine fortune of this Society to be dedicated to patriotism through service to the ideals
of truth, and justice, and beauty as they are revealed in literature and history. Splendid things
it has done, and greater things it is yet to do in
carrying its beliefs into the life of the State.
There is supreme need of a devoted body of loyal
men and women who value material construction,
but upon whom material size of any sort cannot impose. When thousands of strident voices,
organized and unorganized, are every breathing
moment reminding the State of its business and
body, the demand of patriotism is for a militant,
extensive group that will remind it of its soul,
and give somewhat of their lives to that service.

A number of years ago a witty North Carolinian
said that North Carolina was the place where
men still believed in God, read Scott, and voted
the Democratic ticket. That was when skepticism

was more popular, and the Democratic ticket less popular than it is now. But we accept the estimate as indicating the splendid material which challenges patriotic effort in North Carolina: her righteousness, her steadfastness, her beautiful loyalty. No State in the Union offers in the character of its people a more inspiring opportunity for perfecting prosperity in a noble commonwealth through patriotic service to ideal values.

North Carolinians are a truthful people and a truth-loving people. Patriotism urges us to render powerful this native virtue by giving abundant welcome to truth in every practice and activity in our life. Ignorance, with its prejudices, is the great foe to truth, and the warfare we are waging against ignorance is our richest patriotic asset; but no patriotic heart can remain untroubled and inactive when it daily faces the tragic deficiency in our power that comes from the terrible sacrifices that we make to ignorance. Beyond this fundamental service patriotism urges us to energize interest in ideas, to give to knowledge momentum and driving power by sending by all possible means currents of ideas throughout the State. In order to give ideas free course, patriotism urges us to the still higher and more courageous service of creating a free atmosphere of truth. I do not mean truth as I see it, or my party sees it, or my sect of any sort, but truth as it stands revealed to any sincere seeker after it. I mean that for truth to be permanently powerful it must be lifted above its stratified, sectarian stage. Its healthful open-mindedness does not, however, mean indecision and indifference. It believes in its party, in its leaders, in its church. It believes in these things as the practical instruments and exponents of truth to be most valiantly fought for. But it also knows that if the people of a State follow a leader, or a party, or a creed, through fear, mere convention, or a lack of personal concern; speak without sincerity or keep silent through indifference, the vision of truth is sectarian and incomplete—a dead motive; ideas of spiritual construction are thereby blighted, and unable to keep pace with the unchecked freedom of materialism.

A Virginia paper said recently, apropos of corruption in some of our prosperous sister States, that "North Carolina is the cleanest State in the Union." Regardless of whether our merit in this respect is preëminent, it is certainly true that in goodness the nature of our people affords a splendid basis for constructive idealism. I shall not discuss in detail the interesting practical relations that the standard of material prosperity bears to that standard of level, equalized justice that is the life blood of all creative effort of every sort in a free State. I do not mean the standard of technical honesty or stolid righteousness. What I do mean is keeping fresh and vital and dominating the criterion of glowing justice. In establish-

ing this standard over the tyranny of the merely
business standard of success our prosperity has to
face its inexorable problem of the camel and the
eye of the needle.   We shall not build with per-
manence unless in every test between the strong
and the weak—in finance, labor, race, religion,
art, domestic servants—the hundred applications
in legislative and personal practice—we courageously and joyfully make prevail above all other
judgments the standard of glowing justice as the
incarnate conscience of the people.

The editor of *The Progressive Farmer*, who is
also Secretary of the North Carolina Literary and
Historical Association, a combination of offices
that admirably illustrates his interpretation of
successful practice through constructive ideals;
of what I have been trying to say of the passion
for knowing, allied to the passion of making prevail, the union of present business with the business of all time, of devotion to one's own affairs
purified by devotion to the affairs of the State—
this patriotic North Carolinian of faith, has hang-
ing in his remarkable office a reproduction or two
of Raphael's side by side with a reproduction of
Smith's pea planter and Jones's stump puller; a
copy of Emerson's *Essays* is mixed in with a dissertation on subsoil plowing.   I do not know what
Raphael thinks of the crowd he has got into, but I
know that Emerson enjoys it—his robust Ameri-
canism has no prejudices against beauty.

The work of an active people is incomplete without beautiful expression. State life, however prosperous, is nervous, barren, and poverty-stricken, unless it is enriched by noble emotions, nobly expressed and nobly enjoyed. What a benediction in the public life of the State has been our own gray old capitol building, in the gentle perfection of a beautiful age that is ever young—the hallowed memorial of gracious ideals that its presence will not let die. The influence of its beauty on the life of the State has been greater, I suspect, than that of many a chief executive. We do not count the extension of beauty in the form of books, pictures, and architecture as a civic obligation; yet beauty is not less powerful than the sterner virtues in the ideals of a free people.

There are now 2500 rural school libraries scattered over North Carolina, containing 200,000 volumes, in addition to the collections in the larger towns. These should not be cemeteries of dead books, nor mere conveniences for people who already love books, but this society and other agencies that have discovered the beauty of books, should put that beauty into the lives of the people. So our private homes, however simple, have a patriotic service as radiating centers in civic life of the tone and temper of beauty; our municipalities as aggregates, not of competing businesses, but beautiful expressions of the joy of living together. The small towns of which North Carolina is made up offer in their formative stage the best opportunity for growing into the supreme civic grace of beauty—though small towns like small boys are especially careless of their personal loveliness. We prostitute the beauty of our highways of trade to the most vulgar purposes, indifferent to the fact that they, too, are the homes of men, careless of how we build them or build on them. Splendid civic work has been done in the past five years in beautifying our public places, and almost entirely it has been done by women—unfranchised and unfinanced. We need abundantly to welcome this motive of beauty as a dominating ideal into our private and our public construction, making it an active ally in that noble confederation of ideals, that partnership of the present with the past and the future that is the summary of all patriotism, the prophecy of permanent greatness.

May I say, in a word of conclusion, that there are many evidences that while we are building with energy, intelligence, confidence, temples to our god of Industry, that we are stirred by these profounder motives of ideal construction? They are observable in almost every North Carolina town, and nowhere are they more impressive than in our own lately awakened capital city. No other influence could be quite so potent as that there should be here a government not only efficient in practice, but glorifying its practice by illustrations of a genuine civic patriotism that expresses itself by devotedly constructing works of truth, justice, and beauty. But more than any other evidence of a growth of a noble civic faith in North Carolina is that supreme evidence in the life of the people more deeply felt than seen. It is the aspiration, even the yearning of the people of this State for higher things—a passionate docility, combined with the strength of native independence—a yearning for great leadership founded on great principles. Even now these leaders may be waiting. I do not know. The expectation of the people is a compelling prayer. It will be the work of our section, I believe, reëstablished in nationalism through prosperity, to lead the nation out of its confusions of materialism, and it will be only through new interpretations of the old ideals. However this may be, I know that our own heroes will come in commerce, in statecraft, in literature, in religion, when the spiritual temper of the State becomes resurgent through patriotic faith, and so liberates the splendid virtues of constructive materialism from its own unbalanced tyrannies. To usher in this creative era is in part the glorious privilege of every man and woman who would play a patriot's part in the North Carolina of to-day, and achieve in the North Carolina of to-morrow the commonwealth for which men have dreamed and died, but scarcely dared to hope!

HIGHER EDUCATION AND BUSINESS[1]

WHATEVER the question that engages the attention of the thinking educator sooner or later it gets down to the raw product with which he has to deal—the boy; his attitude, his ideals, and the impulses that put him at the door of the college. One of the wittiest of American educators said not long ago that the attitude of the present college boy toward the college faculty was something like this: "You are the educator, I am the educatee. Educate me if you can!"

The remark isn't as witty as it might be, because it isn't true. At least it isn't true as applied to the Southern college boy. His attitude is much more serious—almost too serious we are sometimes surprised into thinking. The product with which we have to deal is eagerly curious to find out what we have to offer and rather nervously anxious to apply that something to a civilization that he is vividly conscious demands of him an unusual contribution.

This prophetic intentness of the Southern stu-

[1] An Address before the Southern Educational Association at Charlotte, N. C., December 29, 1909.

dent is in part responsible for certain impressive characteristics of this educational conference.

No other cause, political, legal, religious, or technical could summon a gathering so interested, so alert, distinguished by such leadership—a conference that in the midst of a national movement that shows signs of disappointment and cynicism, and in the midst of local restrictions that so long baffled and manacled us, is notwithstanding dominated by a mood confident, militant, optimistic —even exhibiting a touch of the triumphant. This mood of the educator like that of the educatee requires comment, and seems to justify large deductions, if we could find them.

One other immediately present consideration fixes my attention: it is the place in which this conference happens to meet.   This is an old town; it was not young when Cornwallis helped to make it historic.   Yet when I played about its streets some fifteen years ago it had not yet awakened into life.   Its streets were country roads; its trading places scarcely better than one-story shanties, its factories, comparatively speaking, non-existent. I cannot walk from the hall where this significant conference holds its meetings to the streets of this town and not know that I am faced with the signs of a fact equally as significant as the fact that is behind this meeting—perhaps is the fact that is behind this meeting.   What one sees here one sees everywhere as the unifying characteristic of the whole section. It takes no eye of the seer to observe it; every chance spectator sees it—a festival pageant of material prosperity. It is garishly hammered into every sense.

I am not about to review the sensational figures of the material revival of the South, and quote per cents that certify wealth to a hitherto penniless section. I merely give momentary emphasis to the revolutionary consequences with which the fact is pregnant, and observe that here again from the confused dissolution of old ideas and prejudices, and from the hazards of new ideas and aspirations there emerges another movement equally with our own, confident, militant, optimistic, with a growing touch of the triumphant. If we achieve the difficult but important task of observing things about us, we cannot fail to see as the two forces that have the remarkable fortune to be dominant in present Southern life: Education and Business.

These two dominant movements unite in a common ultimate task that gives the mood to this meeting, to this town, to every active force in this section; it is the task that fixes the attention of the Southern student and his instructors, as well as the more patently active world about us—the romantic task of commonwealth building that gives to every trade and profession as its dominant motive, construction.

What the quality of this construction will be,

the strength and beauty of the great commonwealths that are rising at our feet, depends in
great measure on the relation of these two dominant forces to each other: whether they build in
opposition, or with indifferent independence, or
in full alliance and sympathy.

It is hardly necessary to analyze fully the state
of present feeling between business and higher
education. Active opposition to higher education
there certainly is not, nor is there active sympathy
and organic coöperation. There is dead conventional acceptance that one is inclined to feel to
be worse than opposition. In the unquestionable
professions of friendship between the two there
is that air of truce and explanation that used to
characterize religion and science. Each emphatically admits the necessity of the other, but with
an accent that suggests regret. Business is satisfied with an occasional contribution vociferously
applauded, according to its size, but the relation is too individual; if I may say it in a word,
too personal, in a matter that is essentially imper-
sonal. Higher education is not the poor relation
of business, nor a graveyard of personal memorials.
Whatever the size of the contribution it is small
compared to what a steadily active interest in the
affairs of the college as a civilization maker would
be. There is not a feeling of equality in the
partnership, there is too much of condescension
in the air of each in a task in which each has

fundamental duties that can be executed only in harmony. To bring this about there should be a vital understanding.

Education needs to comprehend that in this joint commission of commonwealth building the share of business is not merely to create the wealth. The creation of wealth is fundamental in a purely physical sense, and for its liberation of the senses from all of the limitations of poverty and worry; but education needs to understand that the creation of wealth is not merely a stepping-stone to culture and what we call liberal education. We need to realize that the act of creation has high values in the making of a people. To discover them we do not have to search our Emerson for a theoretical doctrine of work, or our Carlyle with his "Destiny has no other way of cultivating us but by our work." If we look about us at the sound, greatly growing things in our present civilization we shall find that the act of creating our wealth is creating our great men. It is easy to point out and identify the cultivating values of the qualities it is giving them: definiteness, courage for details, quickness, confidence, power to organize, the strong ability to realize the opportunities for effective living, equal opportunity for all the people, nationalization. Our business men have discovered in the problems and complexities growing rankly about them a world of realities. Precisely what the value of these qualities is in our present life the limits of this paper prevent illustration and comment. They are liberalizing qualities to be valued and used by a college administration in whatsoever way its own courage and initiative may suggest.

In like manner business needs to comprehend that in this life of large constructiveness higher education is fundamental. Business is cultural; higher education is practical. If business is fundamental for one thing in providing a sound physical basis for life, the highest education is fundamental in providing a sound intellectual basis for life—a basis without which a truly great commercialism cannot exist. Higher education is essential to business for its knowledge-giving power. I hasten to explain that I do not mean for its window displays of the narrow exponents of its technical education—experts in the analysis of cotton-seed oil and iron ore. For these clerkly tasks men are needed and the colleges may turn them out as by-products; but the colleges will make no great claim on our present civilization, even in its most commercial phase, by being absorbed in making them. But a great claim it does make on even the most commercial phase by providing and conserving the highest knowledge that is fundamental in a civilization actively entering into competition with England and New England and Germany. The civilization of North Carolina, Georgia, and Alabama, and the rest, will be founded as elsewhere on university knowledge. Your twelve- or twenty-story building has a firmer foundation than the rock on which it rests; it is the university knowledge that made possible the steel and the cement and the principle of adding eleven towering stories to your self-made one-story that it displaced. That is a material fact and a parable too. Behind the cotton bale on which store and bank and factory rest is the fertilizer that Liebig's discovery made possible.

With the change from a comparatively simple self-supporting individualistic agricultural life to a manufacturing and commercial community, competitive complexity comes as a matter of course, as a matter of consequence from which our present civilization asks for something more than knowledge. It proclaims its insistent demand for men who know how to use that knowledge, and at the same time it certifies its readiness to pay for such men. A business man from Charlotte said a few years ago from the platform at the University of North Carolina that he could place ten men at ten thousand dollars a year in Southern enterprises. And he added bitterly that he couldn't find the men. This maximum efficiency man, this man that can manage men, synthesize knowledge, and master steadily widening fields of knowledge and business that Southern life asks, it will get as its only consistent source of supply from higher education.

These considerations of the relation of business and higher education that steadily widen and deepen as we examine them, though becoming less exact and obvious, lead to one further consideration: business almost loses the name of business as it passes from the first visible act of trade, through the organization and control of trading on out into its state relations, its national and even international relations. Politics and business and higher education have connections intimate and inextricable. Muck-rakers have had a great deal to say about business and politics; they would have had less if higher education had had more. Problems of government, of political science, of sociology, problems of legislating for life growing keener and more necessitous with every quickening sense of material development thrust upon higher education as its final do-this-or-fail obligation that of interpretation and guidance. In the few years just past we have fronted four problems in our civilization that came to the practical issue of decisive voting: free-silver, railway management, prohibition, and tariff. Not even in war were Southern interests so identical; the need for confident far-seeing guidance so insistent; the occasion for great leadership so worthy. We didn't get it, and we announced pretty clearly that we knew we didn't. We made no pretense at being satisfied with what we got when we asked for bread. And we make no con-

cealment of announcing that we have done with
following emotional leadership.   Leaders of a sort
still rally about the faded standards, but the
old battle cries echo drearily across deserted fields.
For present problems we ask for leadership com-
bining the qualities of the two forces in our present
life.   The great commonwealths rising into multiplying powers, conscious of the unwieldiness of
those powers but conscious more of the plenitude
of them, lift their iron lids to the institutions of
light for guidance and light.

But it is living light that they want.   The
ability to supply the State's need is the sole justification of higher education.   It relies on no traditional claims for support; urges no exemptions
or benefit of clergy; is ready to stand or fall by
its fresh, vital service to our present civilization.

Higher educational institutions are the State-
thinking.   Let them be sure that they do think!
To think at all is the most difficult of human
problems; to think of present affairs is the most
difficult phase of thinking.   Our civilization and
its problems and demands are before us.   We
shall find our task first and last there, and not
revealed in any parchment however sagacious,
nor in imitation of any section or institution
however admirable.   We should learn the best
that the best has to teach, but we shall discover
that Massachusetts and Germany are not North
Carolina and Alabama.   Harvard is good and

Hopkins is good, and the Carnegie Foundation is good; we shall listen to them and if need be we shall reject them. For our own, our own we will make better.

A few years ago, some one—Professor James, I think—announced the need in the life of the world for some idea to take the place of war, some romantic passion that would fill the imagination and expand the monotonous activities of daily affairs into heroic proportions. This romantic passion has come to us, in the midst of the industrial democracy of which we are a part, slowly unifying itself in the melting pot of this republic—in our isolated labors, rebuilding at first in bitterness a wrecked civilization we have discovered the abounding joy of commonwealth building, and exhibit to-day the purest and most uplifting phase of the national movement. In answer to the intent youth who stands at our door and knocks we say: "No education is too high for your need; no efficiency too masterful for the enterprises you will be called upon to command; no point of view too wide for leadership in a section potentially great enough to compete with any civilization in the world."

BANKING AND THE LARGER CITIZEN-SHIP[1]

IN speaking on the general subject "Banking and the Larger Citizenship" in a program made up of deliberately specific topics, I would not be accused of purposeless generalities or idealism that cannot be made to work. The subject may not seem as distinctly practical as good roads, good soil, good schools, and yet in thinking as specifically as I can about roads and schools, and even churches that are good, I find that no amount of thinking and talking by public road experts and soil experts and teachers will produce the results we all desire unless along with the specialist knowledge and service that we bring in our line you bring the knowledge and service of yours. I mean that we cannot have good public roads and good public schools unless in addition to good engineering and good teaching we have good public banking and finance. It is to make a simple point in regard to what good public finance is, whether it is practical to have it, and what we can do to further it, that I shall briefly address myself. No question

[1] An Address before the American Bankers' Association at Richmond, Va., October, 1914.

can be of more practical and vital importance than this question of the relation of business and banking to the public welfare, and particularly to the farming public.

The view is current that banking men and business men have no relation except antagonism to the higher and the nobler activities of men. I was reading a day or two ago a sermon by a minister of national reputation and a man of great public spirit, in which this ground was eloquently taken. He reviewed the "awful record of industrial accidents," the ruthless fraud, chicanery, corruption of politics and government by business, the outright robbery honored in the business world, the destruction of our natural resources, on which the nation of the future must live, and he vehemently declared that the only law of business is brute force and the survival of the craftiest. His conclusion from what he had observed in his work is that business is bad in essence and its standards wholly bad.

And this view by constant repetition in pulpit and forum and (up to a few years ago) in the popular magazines convinced even men whose occupation is business that they are a necessary evil in a Christian republic. A good man, they are forced to feel, may be a good man after hours, or on legal holidays, or after he has retired from business. But business is—business. No other word expresses its isolation, its lawlessness, its unrelatedness.

But the typical business man and bank man

(who sits at the center of his alleged game of wealth versus commonwealth) cannot quite believe that this is the whole truth, or even a part of the real truth. Nobody sees so clearly as he that selfishness and greed, strong everywhere that men live and work, are fiercest in business; but he knows that they are *not* business. He acknowledges the power of self-interest and the fierce law of the survival of the crafty; but he knows that it is not the only law, or the great law, and that we are rapidly discovering the higher law even though its standards and demands are not yet quite understood. He looks at the work of his hands and brains—at his factory, his store, his trust company —and it seems to have a place in God's scheme of things. And he looks over this vast country with its giant concerns and institutions of industry and trade—the incarnate expression of the new anti-feudal power of commerce—and it seems, in its work for universal peace, its extension of the suffrage, religious toleration, and diffusion of material well-being, that its contributions to the world's welfare give it a high and noble place in God's scheme of civilization.

He looks about him at the successful men in business, and without analyzing their good qualities, they seem on the whole to measure up to the men in other callings. And more than all of this, whether he achieves the height to which his business calls him or not, the serious business man knows that in his business there is a height that he can spend the best that he has in him in attaining. Often blindly, but with flashes of deeper vision, he feels the thrill of the Creator, and he knows that He, too, is a co-worker with all good men in the building of a Christian commonwealth. He feels that business men who wreck a railway system through financial manipulation are as surely traitors to the whole public as Tweed was or Benedict Arnold; but he feels also that the men who built up the Pennsylvania system, the carrier of the civilization of the people, are quite as worthy workers in the kingdom of righteousness as the artists who designed the plans for its beautiful terminus.

Business is business; but it is also life—an essential part of the life of the individual man and an essential part of the life of the nation. What we are coming to see is that good business, like all other good human activities, has two characteristic marks: It must be a good job in itself and it must be done in accord with the standards of the nation of which it is a part. The first is a question of individual freedom and efficiency, the second is a question of responsibility and relationship. Reconciling their contradictions in a practical standard of Christian democracy is the task of the civilization that we are building. In science, in art, in government our practice conforms to our theory with sufficient clearness to be recognized by all men. No scientist, no artist, no statesman could fail to hold his genius and his profession in large part as public property. Legitimate government by whomever administered is government administered in the interest of the whole body politic. And this standard is coming to be and will be the practical standard of good business.

It is a difficult doctrine, but it is the very thing that is happening before our eyes—this saturation of the standards of business and the uses and processes of business with the national standard. Business responsibility, business self-restraint and coöperation, to the man who really sees, are facts far more significant in present America than ruthless selfishness, greed, and the survival of the craftiest; and the steady progress we are making in a truly democratic interpretation of business is one of the most significant facts in world history.

To the question how we achieved the progress we have made, and how we are to achieve the even more difficult tasks ahead, there is no specific answer. It will not be through legislative panaceas swallowed by Congress and the people suddenly made whole. The lash of legislation cures no business ills, though it may seem, as it does elsewhere, to compel attention to the higher law of self-restraint. Enlightened self-interest has played and will continue to play a large part. But it will be through the same slow and difficult process of self-education by which we learned and are

learning self-government—through realizing more
clearly what we are working for. It is not through
restricting the doctrine that business is business,
but enlarging it to the view that business is life.
We are learning that one may coöperate not only
with a single partner, and a group of partners, and
a group of thousands of dividend sharers; but with
ten thousand workmen and their families, and
that we may extend that vision of partnership to
the whole community and its wealth, health, and
happiness. This insight comes not from conver-
sion to altruistic philanthropy, nor from an out-
burst of emotional patriotism, but through a fuller
knowledge of the facts of public welfare, and so to
a truer conception of our business concerns and
our banking institutions as arteries through which
the life of the community flows, and our bank men
as public men and ministers of the public welfare
as truly as statesmen, teachers, or preachers. When
we know fully and exactly the economic facts
about the public welfare the projecting power of
our practical sympathy will be vastly increased.

Perhaps I can make this clearer by the case of
the Banker Who Discovered an Open Road. He
was a normal sort of person, successful and busy,
and he lived after the fashion of his class. He took
pride in his town and he knew a few things about
it: its rapid growth in population, its fine main
streets, its tax rate, its leading industries. The air
of prosperity that it wore was a daily delight to

him. What he cared most about, of course, was
his bank. He had built it up and put his life into
it. It had grown as the town had grown, and now
it lifted its head proudly to a view of all the wide
country around that it served and was served by.
He knew every detail of its business, and he loved
all of it, down to the fixtures and the bronze plate
in the entry. He had no theories except that he
agreed with Vice-President Marshall in the doctrine of the "clean doorstep"; *i. e.*, he believed that
it was his duty to keep his own doorstep clean
and that that was enough. He did his own job
well, and the question of whether in doing it well
he helped or hindered others in doing their job
well he considered their concern and not his. As
to what doing a job well was he would have referred you to the bank statement. He was not
concerned with public questions except as they
openly touched his interest or the bank's interest,
and he took some pride in the fact that he was not
an "uplifter." The good roads question to him
was a matter of the asphalt avenue that led from
his clean bank steps to the *porte-cochère* of his home.
It went on by, of course, as roads do, but it was
not in his knowledge as to how good or how bad it
was after it was lost in the blue haze of the hill
beyond.

Then in the course of business a simple thing
happened. He acquired a farm nine miles out on
the road. He became interested in it and in

9

making a good job of it, and interested in the tenant and his family, through whom he was to make a good job of it. He found that though you needed good roads, good schools, good churches in your farming community in order to get a good job done there and keep good people there, that it wasn't sheer stupidity and desire for ignorance and unwholesome, unattractive living that kept the people from getting them. He studied the census returns and found that although the people produced a great deal of farm wealth very little of it was economic surplus out of which communities can vote taxes for roads and schools; that they were conducting a business of marketing without a knowledge of marketing, that required coöperation without a medium of coöperating, that they were attempting on a faulty, unorganized credit system to make a profit on a business that between the bank and the store required twelve to twenty per cent. interest. Gradually it came to him that the job at the bank and the job at the farm were parts of the same job precisely, and that both are vital organs in the same healthful community life. The bank was no longer an isolated enterprise, but in its being at the heart of the community's material affairs vitally affected every public activity.

What he discovered through learning some facts of public welfare was not that he had before been a bad man with a bad business, but that his job was a vastly bigger and more inspiring job than he had understood. He knew what it was to be a bank man; he discovered what it was to be a man in the bank. He knew that the public street was a satisfactory way downtown and back; he found that the same street was an open road to the end of the world. He found that what the standards of his country asked of him was not that he sacrifice himself and his business in sentimental service, but that he liberate himself and it through exercising freely the privileges of the larger citizenship.

Because we believe that knowing about the facts of our whole community life is the first step in dealing fairly and generously with them we have instituted in North Carolina a state-wide campaign for arousing non-partisan interest in the state of the public welfare. The first step in this campaign is a Community Service Week decreed a few days ago by proclamation of the Governor to be celebrated all over the State the first three days in December. The first of these days is a "Public Roads, Grounds, and Buildings Day," on which the men and women and young people of each town, township, or school district will meet according to plan and work together in one of three forms of actual physical service to the community: (1) in making more worthy and creditable streets and roads; (2) in improving the exterior and interior of public buildings; (3) in beautifying school

grounds, cemeteries, parks, and planting trees, etc.,
along the streets, roadsides, and private grounds.
The second day is "School and Neighborhood
Improvement Day," with the neighborhood served
by the school as the unit, and on this day meetings
will be held in the schoolhouses to discuss community conditions, ways for improving social life,
economic and health conditions, and committees
will be named to prosecute plans for carrying out
the ideas suggested. The third day is "County
Progress Day," on which a great public meeting
shall be held at each county seat to discuss the
needs and possibilities of the county in the light
of comparisons made with the conditions in the
county ten years before and with conditions in
other counties. Careful and detailed programs for
each of these days, with abundant and specific
information, have been prepared in the form of a
civic handbook by a central committee, a plan of
organization for each county outlined in the fashion
of organizing a political campaign, a paid secretary
employed to conduct the campaign from the State
capitol.

At the State University we are putting this idea
of local, applied economics and civics directly into
the curriculum and activities. Our students are
largely North Carolinians. Groups of them come
from every county in the State. These are organized into county clubs, and these clubs federated into a State club, in which the studies that

the county clubs make of local conditions are compared with each other and set over against the conditions in other States. These studies are based on a syllabus prepared by the professor of rural economics and sociology of the University, who gives his whole time to this work, summing up county conditions from investigations of population, wealth, domestic animals, coöperative enterprises, public highways, law and order, recreation, rural credit, churches, marketing, and home conditions.

We believe that in a democratic commonwealth such as ours, no matter what our method of approach is—whether through banking, education, manufacturing, farming—a primary condition in promoting the sort of progress that we are all at heart agreed on wanting is a more thorough knowledge of what the facts are. With this will come freer and less prejudiced discussion, a deeper and truer understanding of the principles underlying the facts and a practice that will accord to a more generous and human interpretation of them. Our great lesson, bitterly hard to learn, but holding the infinite secret of individual and national freedom that we seek, and the great lesson that we will learn, is that these streets and stores, and fields, and banks, and factories, and schoolhouses, and churches, and all the rest, are but "folds across the face of God" and that the "Thy will" for which we daily pray will be done here and now or nowhere;

and that banking, agriculture, education, freedom, and life itself are but instruments for finding the common God in the common good and making through our daily task His will prevail.

III

STUDENT AND COLLEGE
RELATIONS

THE COLLEGE AND HUMAN NEED[1]

WE begin to-day what gives promise of being the greatest year in the almost century and a quarter of the University's history. All of the factors in a vigorous and healthy life are actively and consciously coöperating in its support. It has the respect of its sister institutions throughout the country, the confidence and esteem of the people of the State, the enthusiastic loyalty of its alumni, and the intelligent and whole-hearted love of its rapidly growing student body.

It is not unnatural that we should rejoice in its growing strength and size and, conscious that no compromise of any standard has been made, we have no disposition to apologize for this evidence of its success. There are those who advocate the superior virtue of a small college, and certainly none of us here confuses mere bulk and true greatness. Smallness has its associated virtues. I do not need to name them. Growth has its problems. Switzerland is an admirable country in its fine way. It has many advantages not possessed by the

[1] An Address before the Student Body at the Opening of the University of North Carolina, September, 1915.

137

United States.   It is untroubled by many of the
complex problems that vex this great country.   I
should not argue, however, that it is great because
it is small, nor hope for any sound conclusions from
an argument founded on its miniature and fixed
proportions.

I trust that the time will never come when we
shall rejoice in size for its own sake, nor sacrifice a
detail of our standards for the sake of false growth;
but I do rejoice that the University of North Carolina reflects in its growth a well-proportioned and
vigorous life, and reflects the steadily increasing
interest of the State in education, carrying with
it, as evidenced by your presence here, the endorse-
ment of every section, of every vocation and profession, of every degree of poverty and wealth.
We believe too much in what it stands for, not to
rejoice that so many of the people of the State
believe in what it stands for.   It gives us courage,
faith, and aggressive purpose to go about widening
and deepening the saving influences of the permanently great things it lives to promote.

I said a moment ago that the true greatness of
the University, and the reality of its progress does
not depend on its size.   I should like to put to you
the question: Upon what does its true greatness
depend? and the corollary question: Upon what
does your success here, and your own greatness as
a University student depend?   We shall not make
much progress until we get some clear and intelli-

gent approach to an answer to these questions. Whether we get an answer in the few moments that I shall ask you to consider them now, we may make a start toward an answer that the year will make clearer.

The answer that I give, I offer without preliminary: The greatness of a college depends upon its ability to satisfy the supreme human need of the people and time it serves. The life and health of a college are not mysterious. Colleges have a way of dying and going to seed; they have a way, as the years go by and take toll of their vitality, of losing their fruitful impulse, and becoming a set of more or less worthy and dignified by-laws. The great college is the college that supplies the civilization it serves with a program of guidance—a way out of the difficulties through which the people are trying to find their way, and equips its students to be representative men in the era in which they live. Colleges have risen to greatness as they have done this, and they have fallen away as they have merely repeated in mechanical routine traditional exercises that are off the key of the master note of their own time.

It would not be difficult to show, I think, how great institutions have been as naturally the outgrowth of the life of the people they served, as the trees of the soil, and how they represent the successively great ideas and ideals that man in his slow progress through the centuries has evolved. They

have realized for men the new life relations that
men at work have been steadily trying to discover,
and have equipped young men to interpret these
relations through their professions—the Universities of Paris, Salerno, Bologna, Oxford, Berlin, the
great technical schools of Europe, and, in our own
country, Harvard, Hopkins, and the great state
universities.   They stood and stand for some
supreme human need in the successive stages of
advancing civilization—ecclesiasticism, culture,
science. Their training has in each case been professional and practical, guiding the needed idea
into fruitful interpretation, and training the representative man of the time: the hero-type,
whether he was the churchman, the statesman, the
courtier, the man of science, or what not. What is
important, then, to the greatness of our college,
and to you, is that the college should patiently and
passionately seek to know what the supreme need
of our time is, and after seeing that need as clearly
as it can, resolutely to satisfy it.

It is a commonplace—and I state it in its baldest
form—to say that the time we live in is above all
else a practical time. It is called commercial. It
is even said to have sold out humanity's great ideas
and ideals to dollar standards of success; and it
is further said that education, and particularly
college education, has lost its permanent values
through becoming superficial and practical.

College education has become obviously practical in its tendencies. This is shown not only by the upgrowth of specifically technical schools, but by the whole college curriculum. It is shown in our own curriculum by the courses called "B. S. Med."; the combined A. B. and law course; the numerous engineering courses, in which students at entrance definitely set out on the trail of their professions. But it is not true that the real values of college training have been set at naught by this vocational inclination, nor is it wise in my judgment for the college to belittle practical values, nor lament the lack of worship at its ancient shrines. What it must do is to make convincingly clear how wholly essential to present practical life its permanent truths and methods are.

The scientific revolution of the nineteenth century gave a new framework to human thinking and to human conduct. It created a century that is a wonderful chapter in the history of the race. It was inevitable, too, that this great period was to be followed by a period of application, in which the wonders of science and invention would be translated into practice and give once again a new framework to our thinking and our conduct, our material welfare, and, through revolutionized conditions of human associations of free men at work in a world of industry, give us a new philosophy of living and a new social conscience.

This application of the world's knowledge to the everyday practical concerns of men has not lost or lowered any standard of learning. It has, as President Goodnow has said, made the engineer out of the mechanic, the architect out of the carpenter, the naval constructor out of the boat builder. It has interpreted human labor in terms of intelligence; it has liberated human hands and minds; and it has liberated wealth for human comfort and enjoyment. The problem of modern university education is not to combat the application of abstract truth and the mastery of how to do in addition to what to know—as religion and culture combated the coming of science. Behind the practical, material, and commercial standards of the new social order that is in the process of construction, there is an idealism that it is the unique obligation of higher education to stimulate and interpret in our everyday life. The activities of men have taken a new shift, but the single great art, as Professor H. B. Adams has recently said, is now as always the art of living.

It is in giving a new and higher interpretation to making a living under a broader interpretation of a better art of living for all of the people, that the college finds its great present task. It is a task that does not discard the ideals of culture or the methods of truth for its own sake. For its ideals to be permanent, they must be founded on the ideals that men have wrung from experience, and must include them. To untangle the web of materialism and liberate idealism through a mastery of its deeper human relations is the task that gives to universities—I am paraphrasing Professor Adams again—an opportunity such as never before existed in the history of the world. It is upon their mastery through education of the practical world of vocation, and upon their ability to saturate efficiency in making a good living with the ideals of living a good life that the greatness of a modern university depends. The representative man, the product of such a university, may be a great churchman, a great soldier, a great statesman, a great scientist, but he will preëminently be a great citizen.

Your own success here and your greatness as a college student, if I may so phrase it, depends on your ability to train yourself through your quiet days of study here in those qualities that will be demanded of this representative man in the world in which you are preparing to take your place.

May I briefly trace what these qualities seem to me necessarily to be. First: No student is truly trained unless he has learned to do pleasantly, and promptly, and with clean-cut accuracy every task he has obligated himself to do. A man may decline to undertake a job, but to undertake it and shirk it is a crime in the world of efficiency. An undergraduate has said that the main purpose of colleges seems to be to give students incapacity for work. This is because some students dodge every duty to which the death penalty is not attached, and train themselves into the fatal habit

of doing as they like. I presume that it is the pre-
valence in colleges of these amiable conspiracies
for making indolence respectable that has caused
that master workman, Mr. Henry Ford, to em-
ploy no college men in his factory. Decisive and
purposeful performance of every duty is a fundamental rule of success in life that no man has
the right to train himself away from in college.

Second: No student is truly trained unless, in
addition to getting this mastery of the tools of life
that comes through the discipline of routine tasks,
he puts into his work his own personal curiosities
and opens his faculties to a lively and original
interest in his work that leads him to test for himself what he is told. Every subject lends itself to
this spirit of inquiry, and no subject has real fruitage until it has in some way, small or great, had its
conclusions retested, and its truths rediscovered
by the student himself.

Third: No student has been truly trained unless,
in addition to learning to do a workmanlike job,
and cultivating a lively spirit of insistent inquiry,
he also gets from his contact with the master
spirits of the race those qualities of taste and be-
havior and standards of judgment that constitute
a true gentleman. "To have spent one's youth at
college," says William James, "in contact with the
choice and rare and precious, yet be a blind prig or
vulgarian, unable to scent out human excellence,
or divine it amid its accidents, to know it only

when labeled and forced on us by others, this indeed should be accounted the very calamity and shipwreck of a higher education."

Fourth: In addition to these individual interests, no student is truly trained unless he realizes that he does not live to himself alone, but is a part of an organic community life that is the source of most of the privileges he enjoys. He is and will ever be a member of a social group that implies responsibilities and services to it quite as important as those he owes to himself. These he may learn with unusual force and intimacy in the fine loyalties of a college community. What the total power and spirit of the college will be is affected by every detail of the conduct of each individual that composes it, the tone of its atmosphere by every man that breathes it.

There is nothing mysterious about the part the college will play in giving you the qualities that will equip you for this great adventure on which you are setting out. She cannot, by allowing you to room within sight of the well, nor by any system of examinations or lectures, give you a single virtue, nor has she a wishing cap by which she can "wish on you" any capacity or quality that you do not have. Before she can answer your inquiry as to what she means to say to you as your foster mother, she asks you a very simple question. It is, "What do you want; and what are you willing to pay?" You may remember in your mythology, and in your Grimm's fairy tales, that when the hero's fortune was so great that the kind fairies put themselves at his service, they always asked him what he wanted. He had at least to *choose*. It was the way with the wonderful youth Solomon. It is the way with you, O wonderful youth, whoever you are, that have come to this fairy godmother of modern times: She will mean to you what you will, and what you will she will give it to you. I should like to make this splendidly clear, and take the full responsibility for the promise: the college will give to you this year whatever gift you seriously ask of her. I challenge you, therefore, to answer with a choice, and I call upon you to consider with all intentness and manly intelligence what your momentous choice is, and that you put behind that choice, once made, every ounce of power you possess!

I have not talked to you of discipline and rules, nor of the great traditions that through the century have hallowed this spot, created by the loving care and sacrifice of the splendid company that have gone before you in this institution. I assume that its traditions are as precious to you as they are to me, and I commit them to you, whose heritage they are, in absolute confidence that you will not only keep the faith, but transmit it to those who come after you with its light heightened and brightened. I assume that you will be jealous of the honor of this college, and guard it as you would that of your mother. I do not emphasize the negative virtues of the boy, but the positive virtues of the man. You aren't here merely to live a life of stagnant goodness; you have come here, because you have "come to yourself," and to answer the thirst of your awakened self for capable and distinguished achievement. If you have, you will set for yourself no standard of mediocrity, nor subscribe to any cult of the second best in your studies, your interests, your tastes, and your companions. If you have come with such a manly impulse, I urge you not to compromise it in a single detail. There is but one real tragedy that can happen to you now or hereafter, and that is deliberately to abandon your ideals. Whatever contribution this college makes to the progress of men will come from your valiant pursuit of your ideals while you study here, and from your clear understanding of the identity of your interests with the interests of the college.

This college should be and can be the most conspicuous achievement of this people. "It can be more influential in making actual the dormant and inactive ideals of the State than any institution in the world has been—more serviceable, more admirable—a genuine triumph of youth and self-mastery, efficient training, and self-government."

I commit it to you: the ark of the covenant of the fathers, your infinitely priceless present possession, the saving hope and heritage of your children and their children's children.

THE SPIRIT OF THE UNIVERSITY[1]

WE meet to-day not only to welcome you here, but to pay recognition to the true significance of your coming. The sense of joy that the college feels in having you here, and the stirring sense of pride that she feels in having so great a throng of you for her sons has a deeper source than the mere happiness of association. What seems important at this moment to you and to me, and compels our attention as I think of you and face you as a group, —and as individual persons, infinitely confident, strong, lovable, ambitious,—is what it is that has brought you here away from the shops, the fields, the sea, the streets, where the vast majority of men of your age are making the grim struggle for success in the rough terms of actual life; what it is that you have put your faith in that has led you to come and enlist for four precious years under this standard.

It has been one hundred and twenty-one years since Hinton James, the first student here, made the journey that each of you has just made. What he found here was chiefly and I may say solely the

[1] An Address before the Student Body at the Opening of the University of North Carolina, September, 1916.

148

Presiding Professor, Dr. David Ker, who had been waiting for a month for the first student to come. When James finally arrived, I have no doubt that the President assembled him at once and gave him some excellent advice. Without any information whatever on the subject, I will venture to say what it was. He told him that he was at a critical time in his career, that he enjoyed opportunities not enjoyed by other young men, that the country was also in a peculiarly critical situation, and that it looked to the college men to save it!

All of which I take to be perfectly true. Every age is a critical age to a thing that has life, and especially so to a young man who feels the surge of abounding life in every limb. Seventeen hundred and ninety-five was a wonderfully critical year in the life of the University, of this country, and the world at large, and especially in the life of the youth Hinton James, as he came here asking the way of life. But not more wonderfully critical, I am sure, than the year 1916–17, to the world, to you, and to me. And so it has been always and will be to every young man as he gathers up his strength and faces the world with it—to Cain, to Samuel, to Absalom, to David—to the young man who came to the Master by night, asking the true way to life; just as it has been to the unending procession of eager-hearted young men who have followed Hinton James through these halls, and with the same question in their hearts, if not on their lips.

I do not know what Hinton James thought of what the President said. Students here seem always to be normally hospitable toward listening to advice, and abnormally sensible about forgetting as much of it as they don't care for.

Being a freshman James may have felt that the President needn't worry about the country (someone has said that a college ought to be a wonderfully wise place—that freshmen bring such a lot of knowledge, and the seniors never take any away); that he could look after the country in his odd moments if the President would only tell him what there was going on now to keep a fellow from being bored to death.

Or, if he was not possessed of this confident spirit of "let Hinton do it," he may have been of that other type that has no reaction whatever to the sharp challenge of opportunity and the appeal for a critical decision. He may have been like the darkey who passed a factory as the whistles were blowing for the critical hour of dinner: "Blow, blow," he said, with calm resignation to his fate. "Dinner time for some folks; but 'taint nothin' but twelve o'clock for me!"

There is plenty of evidence that James was keenly alive to the opportunities offered him: he had an honorable college career and an after career that was an honor to the college; but if I knew nothing whatever of his record I could say with assurance two simple things about him, as I think

I can about you or any other average college man:
(1) He wants to enjoy his youth, and gratify the
thirst for use that every muscle and pore of his
growing body craves.   Life through a hundred
keys of interest appeals to him, and above them
all he holds a sort of fierce, invincible belief that
he has the right to immediate happiness.   There
wasn't anybody here in 1795 but Doctor Ker and
Hinton and the Davie Poplar, but one of the first
things the boy did was to write an essay on "The
Pleasures of College Life."   But he also wrote one
on "The Uses of the Sun," and another on "The
Effect of Climate on Human Life."

And that suggests the other thing that I would
know I could say about him or any other young
man coming to college: (2) He not only wants to
enjoy to the full the youthful physical life that is
his only once; but also he wants to realize the more
keenly felt, though less clearly defined passion for
something of larger, freer use, more deeply rooted,
of more permanent satisfaction.   Through the
eating, drinking, and sleeping of every day, the
buttoning and unbuttoning routine of existence,
this deeper life of the mind and spirit sends up
signals of its hopes and dreams, asking for expression and liberation and to get born through
him in great forms of useful work, science or art.
Every man feels that passion as really as he does
the other.   It is the eternal essence of his manhood.   There is something in him of the Prodigal,

of Esau and of Saul—the men who sold out for a price they could clutch—who swapped their star dust for common clay; there is something also of the Prodigal and Paul—the men who claimed their birthright back, who "came to *themselves*" and came back. Every young man's life is an unprecipitated solution of all biography: of Nero, Benedict Arnold, and Jess Willard; but no less of Socrates, Shakespeare, Newton, Washington, Lincoln, Lee, Pasteur.

Every college man recognizes these two clear calls to him, and most men feel that in the ordinary life of every day there is a sharp contradiction between them: that there must be a surrender of one of them, that college life at best must be a compromise between one's youth and his maturity, what he is now and what he wants to be fifteen years from now—a truce between his happiness and his ambition.

Now it is at this point, I think, that the college speaks its great word, and speaks the one that you have come to ask it to speak. You may think that you have come to ask it how to get into medicine, or how to make money, or how to make an N. C. sweater or a Phi Beta Kappa key, or how to be an engineer, or how to get into society—or any other of the one thousand things that men work and die for. These are understandable motives for coming to college, and the college incidentally can respond to them all; but it could not answer them successfully if there were no deeper motive behind them. The great question that you bring to the University to-day has a deeper center than a desire for either physical satisfaction or success in the world. It is the question that the young man came to the Master with—"What shall I do to inherit life"—the larger, abundant life that will satisfy all of the finer passions of my life.

The Master made this young man a fairly easy answer. He told him, for one thing, to play the game according to the rules laid down. The young man replied that he had always done that. Then the Master shifted the whole point of view to the heart of the mystery. He told him that the source of life is not a set of "rules, a ceremonial, a doctrine, an organization; but an attitude, an atmosphere, a life."

And the answer of the University to your question—as the answer of the greatest of human institutions to the greatest of human questions—is the same as that of the Master.

It answers, play the game according to the rules; but it, too, adds that this is only incidental. The education that it offers you is not in reality a mass of facts, a degree, a curriculum. Above and beyond all of that it, too, is an attitude, an atmosphere, a way of life. It is the way of life based on the innate passion for the intelligent way of doing things. It is the intellectual way of life, and it declares that curiosity, the spirit of free inquiry, the passion to know, is as natural in a human being as the desire to breathe or to eat. It declares its faith in the controlling power of the mind to find the best path in the confusions that beset a man's path, and "its superiority in contrast with every other power, and in its technique, because it can be applied to every undertaking not only in studies, but in industry, in public life, in business, in sport, in politics, in society and religion."

To become a true University man it is necessary to come into this way of looking at things. It does not mean the abandonment of any legitimate sort of happiness whatsoever, nor the loss of any freedom. The adventure of discovering and liberating one's mind, far from being a dull and dreary performance, is the most thrilling of all youthful adventures. There is no question of self-punishment or external discipline; but only the freedom of becoming one's own master, instead of a slave to the tyranny of one's low and cheap desires. To come into this insight is to see this organized discovery of the mind that we call education, not as learning, but as a love of knowledge, not as a matter of being industrious, but of loving industry, not as a matter of giving us a good start toward a middle-age success, but to enable us to keep growing, and so lay hold on the eternal spring of life. What the University stands for is this natural loyalty to truth, to work, to life at its fullest and best that comes through the intellectual way of

life. Its faith is that through that way it may lead
men into the richest and most abundant expression
of their best selves. Its mission, therefore, is to
lead them to come to themselves in the highest
degree, and so through whatever happy travail of
spirit to be "born again." In this way, the University is truly our Alma Mater—mother of the
best in men.

True college or University spirit is generated out
of that, and can have no other source. Its central
concern is a quick and eager interest in ideas, and
its temper a radiant enthusiasm for human excellence in all human pursuits. Consequently it
stands not only for efficiency and excellence in
studies, but for excellence in sports, in dress, in
language, in manners; in sport, not as victory
alone—though the doctrine of human excellence
insists on that,—but sportsmanship; in conduct,
not on honesty alone, but honor. Nothing that
interests a man is foreign to its point of view of
present efficiency, steadily growing into the durable
success and the happiness of an intelligently developed and complete life.

It is not necessary to go to college to get this attitude of eager interest in the intelligent way of life.
Many men outside of college walls have been true
university men; and many men inside have been
dead to its message. Horace Greeley had a sign
outside the *Tribune* office: "No college men or
other horned cattle need apply." The Almighty

has no prejudice for mere college graduates; nor has the world. They have no permanent prejudices, except for the superior over the inferior. They ask not for men who are college men with a blind and sentimental passion to serve; but for men whose intelligent way of life has equipped them as superior agencies for doing the work of the world.

The beginning of this great year finds you facing the world at a moment of extraordinary interest and inspiration to men as individuals, as citizens of the State and of the world. "The immediate future," said President Wilson the other day, "brings us squarely face to face with many exacting problems, requiring new thinking, fresh courage, and resourcefulness . . . stimulating us to the display of the best powers within us." In this splendid trial by battle of what men live by, you belong to the most privileged—I may say, the only privileged class in the world—not in that you are registered in a college, but in that you are permitted under the best conditions to work freely, loyally, and wholly for all that men hold precious. I have every confidence that in this splendid business, you will so take your part that this year will mark a great and definite step in your individual growth, and make of this spot and of this institution the birthplace and mother of that best product of any civilization — masterful, intelligent men, eternally and invincibly loyal to their highest natures.

THE UNIVERSITY AND THE WAR[1]

I SPEAK to you briefly on behalf of the University, and my first word for her is a simple word of complete and hearty welcome, and of grateful happiness that henceforth she is to be truly the mother of you all, united through her in a common high interest and purpose, and also through her drawn into fellowship with that gallant company of men who for a century and a quarter have preceded you here.

For the University, these first formal moments of opening are always moments of her greatest happiness, because they mark the birth of a new generation of University men, with renewed assurances of the precious loyalties and affection that grow out of the association. It is a natural and altogether worthy impulse to open one's heart wholly to the fine feeling of comradeship that draws us together, and to give our mind, for a moment or two, to its meaning—perhaps to define for the present year what that meaning is, in the especial interests that should now enlist the loyalties of men who are the heirs of great traditions.

[1] An Address before the Student Body at the Opening of the University of North Carolina, September, 1917.

157

The attempt to discover just where in our present time and place we stand—always important and sometimes interesting—is especially important this year. Just how critical the particular point of light is that falls on the young men of this year of grace 1917, I hardly dare attempt to say. . . . When Destiny focuses on the hour in which one chances to come into the full strength of youth, the most terrific impact of destruction that history has ever known, or can know, nature mercifully withholds from us the imagination to conceive it. You are perhaps too acutely conscious of the change to submit to a description of it. I am talking to men who for three years have heard the devastating storm of a world in arms grow steadily closer and closer, and have finally seen it break, terrible but not unwelcome, over their own homes, and into the seclusion of this quiet place. Life has been transformed from a pleasantly far-off future of your own choosing to a present made grimly terrible by a job of death that desperately cries for all the disciplined manhood and resources that the world can muster.

At such a time for us to meet here in the shade of these trees, to take up the old studies in the same old way of pleasantness and peace, would seem unworthy and even grotesque. Odd if for us old things in some deep, true way did not become new. If under such compelling summons the University spirit and your spirit here were still the same, you

might resent it with all the ardor of your soul.
But we know that—whether yet directed to any
real end of helpfulness or not—we know that our
attitude is not the same.   For even the most
thoughtless (I hope you will be quietly testing in
your own mind what I am saying) there is in the
place of listlessness, slackness, and indifference, a
desire, however vague, to play a man's part in
a man's world; even to the most vacant mind,
a strong inner voice of awakened mastery, calling, though the direction may be as yet undefined.
Not in vain has the world been echoing these three
years with the tramp of men who march to death,
and gladly

>   .   .   .   pour out the red,
> Sweet wine of youth; give up the years to be;
> Of work and joy, and that unhoped serene,
> That men call age.

Great issues and the scent of heroism and of fellowship with it, and with its vision and its sacrifice,
fill the mind and heart, and call the will of every
true man to some sort of resolution that shall take
the form of action.   The world is aflame, not merely
with the destruction and the anguish of war, but
aflame, too, with a new purpose and luminous with
a great new hope.

With all of these aspirations this immortal
mother of yours is in full understanding and sympathy.   Your vision is her vision.   Her tempered

wisdom looks at the world through the eager eyes and ardent hopes of you, her present sons—and she is as you would have her,

Young as the age in which she lives, fresh as the year of grace in which you come to her, new as all the forces now blowing across the face of the world—running ahead, and showing us the way, with the light lifted high, shining on the path beyond.

So when the call of this great war came, in her quick and eager response, she was first among the first. Three hundred and more of her sons hurried to the first training camps; and for every service since, men who have sat where you sit now were quick to volunteer.

It has always been so. It is the logic of her life and history. The first thing that caught your eye here was the bronze figure of the young soldier in the center of the campus in memory of the great company of young men who left this place desolate in the 60's, and "joyfully," as has been said, "stormed at all the thousand doors that lead to death." In that great conflict no institution, on either side of the line, gave a larger per cent. of its students. Mr. Connor told the wonderful story here this summer. Yale gave 25 per cent.; Virginia, 25; North Carolina, 40, and of its younger alumni, 55.6 per cent. The whole student body pressed into service, and, as one historian states, "rushed into the struggle like men bidden to a marriage feast." Mr. Connor tells, too, the thrilling tale of how at Gettysburg Colonel Isaac Avery, a member of the class of 1847, led General Hoke's brigade across an open field, captured one hundred prisoners and four standards, but was himself killed. Struck down while cheering on his men, he lived long enough to write on an envelope, crimson with his blood, this message: "Tell my father I died with my face to the foe."

This message, a transcript from the heart of the University through one of her sons, was shown to Ambassador James Bryce. He looked at it and said: "It is the message of our race to the world." And it is the message and the spirit of the race of men who "would be free or die," given to you through the University to-day.

Your Alma Mater does not say to you that you are here in her sheltering care to save yourselves while others die, nor because you are too good for the trenches, nor that you are in preparation here for jobs that death will soon make vacant. If she did, you might well be resentfully impatient, and decline to let your strength wither in playing so empty a rôle.

The University holds no such negative view of what we are called upon to be and do here during the next nine months. Our part, if truly conceived and heroically done, is as important, and I dare say as difficult, as that of the men in the trenches. In fact, the vision that they gladly die for, is simply this life of freedom left in trust to us, as trustees of the world's greatest vision, while they fight for its full preservation. The faith for which the world is now being tested out in a crucible of fire is the *faith that with the right to live freely, men will live rightly;* that with a free choice between the inferior and the superior, free men will choose the better way; and that knowledge and power to choose rightly in any activity, and the continuous purpose to carry out the choice, *come from within*. True sovereignty ultimately is within the individual man, or nowhere.

This vision, which is the central impulse and guide of all permanent progress, did not come first to men in August, 1914, nor April, 1917; but because in 1914 a powerful nation, through faith in another great and fatally antagonistic idea, perfected in the discipline of autocratic power and efficient organization, threatened the concept of freedom that we hold in common with the free spirit of half the world, we threw all of our resources of life and treasure into the struggle, that "government of the people and for the people should not perish from the earth." *This issue of freedom is the only issue* in this immediate and terrible task of those who "would be free or die." And the simple point that I would give emphasis to now is that the essential and ultimate victory against autocracy is not this victory against Germany—immediately necessary as that is. The essential victory is not for democracy in government merely. Government exists, not as an end in itself, but to make right conditions for right living. The essential and ultimate fight is for that method of living that will produce the best life; and *justification by practice* of that declaration of democracy that the best way is the *self-directed way*, and *not* the way of outside force, however enlightened: of divine right of family, or caste, or might—militaristic or otherwise. This war has summoned into superhuman effort all of the energies of men, as the President has said in his definitive phrase, simply to "make the world safe" for that ultimate experiment— to carry on *without interference* the experiment of *disciplining ourselves*, and so disciplining ourselves that we will achieve the most abundant physical, mental, and spiritual life. That is the ultimate fight—*whether men can discipline themselves*—and that is the fight that is to test the vision of freedom that has led men through the centuries to fight and fail and fight on, and gladly, if they still might pass on the torch, "die with their face to the foe." And that ultimate task and supreme experiment is what is left with us here for these nine months, *as trustees of freedom to try out under conditions practically ideal.*

As a matter of actual belief and working faith, a great many men in this country (in this town and in this hall, no doubt) believe that this experiment is destined to failure, for the reason that men are not capable of self-discipline,—that they never have been strong enough for it, and never will be. The autocracy of foes within,—indolence, trivial self-indulgence,—the host of petty enemies in the day's battle line have often been too strong for the self-governing average man. Certainly it is easier for some men to charge through barbed wire on the cold steel of German bayonets than to crawl out of a warm bed on a February morning to attend a first-hour Math. class. Yet the whole problem of democratic civilization is symbolized in this test of whether when the obviously right thing to do presents itself, the intelligent free man will choose it, and be strong enough to do it. We are fighting Germany for the privilege of staying in bed if we want to; but the victory of democracy will not be won unless when we win the right to stay in bed we choose to get up, when it's best to do it.

I suspect that in the severe self-appraisal through which the world has been forced in the past three years, the discipline of militaristic compulsion of Germany has superficially won more converts as a practical scheme of effective living than our method of democratic freedom.

I remember hearing not long ago a distinguished college president say that "there are but two kinds of discipline,—military discipline and no discipline." He meant that however safe the world might be for democracy, democracy was not safe for college men.

I had a letter the other day from the father of an entering student, asking if we were to have enough military work here to make a man of his son. He meant, if I may irreverently put it so, to ask if we were to so tie him to tasks that he would be deprived of the inalienable right of every free man to make a fool of himself. In his judgment this young man is not a fit trustee for democracy's vision.

We should frankly face and confess our failures in the past, as we grapple with the task we mean to undertake. Our men at Oglethorpe repeatedly wrote to me this summer: "This work is hard. I do not know whether I can stand it, and whether I can win my commission; but I do know it's making a man of me. I've always wanted to see if I could do it." *Under compulsion* they subordinated all of those petty indulgencies and weak complaints that had hitherto dominated their aspirations to lead a clean, clear-cut, masterful, and purposeful life.

They meant that they were forced to correct those deficiencies that they had previously been too weak to prevent, as pointed out in the letter of General McCain, commenting on the failure of men in the training camps.

That is what the world wants, whether in the army, in athletics, in business, or in scholarship: absence of slouchiness, mental and physical slackness, indifference in thought and bearing, content

with second-rateness. To win that is to win the
fine, heroic fight that falls to us.

But "to walk and carry oneself in all things with
the bearing of a gentleman" means to walk self-
supported, without braces. The absolutism of
militaristic Germany does not give what we have
failed to get. General Pershing said that he hoped
the American army training camps would somehow preserve that invaluable quality of initiative
and self-confidence that American college men get
in football training. The self-imposed discipline
and sportsmanship of the athletic field for the joy
of the game is something like it,—the relentless
regularity and reliability of a machine, combined
with the infinitely varied capacities of the individual spirit: the organized discipline of Germany
and the soul of France. That is the vision of freedom that it is not visionary to expect to dominate
an American university campus in the year 1917.
And that is the vision and the practice that must
dominate our campus if we are to be faithful to
the sacred trust committed to us. Surely if this
reveille of the spirit that has stirred the wide world
to endure mangled bodies that we might still be
strong to carry the message on; sightless eyes that
we might still follow the light; death in its most
hideous forms that we might live more abundantly
—surely at such a time for a man not to raise his
energies to their highest power for the part of the
great job assigned to him is to be a slacker of the

most despicable type. There is no room in this or
any other vital institution in the world to-day for
neutrality in this high endeavor. To be a loafer
to-day is to be not only disloyal to our country, but
to commit the unpardonable sin of being a traitor
to life itself. In this supreme experiment of freedom, we need for our part the same exultant
determination that stayed with Avery to the
death.

Does the University have too much faith in you
when it commits this vision of democracy into your
keeping? I have another letter on my desk in
which the father of one of you says: "Do not these
University students have too much freedom?"
To that, the University answers that it has no faith
not based on full, complete, wholehearted faith
in her sons. That faith is her life as it is the life of
the world. And as it knows they would face death
in a righteous cause with gladness; so it would have
them face exactions of a disciplined life of freedom
—not solemnly, but as a race of confident, up-
standing, masterful, *happy* men—who know how
to live an ordinary life in an extraordinary way,
filled with that heroism for the daily task that
marks the only true chivalry—the chivalry of the
spirit. There is every reason why such men should
go into the great fight for self-disciplined freedom
like the minstrel of old—with a song of victory on
their lips. This is that "league of honor, that partnership of opinion" of which the President spoke

in April, "through which a free people, and only a free people, can hold their purpose steady to a common end not only in their own interest but in the interest of all mankind."

STUDENT LIFE AND CONDUCT[1]

THE romance of college life that clusters about
the more or less amiable law-breaking and irre-
sponsibility of a decade or two ago, does not exist
any more as a feature of the college scene. If one
wants college local color, he will find little of it in
present college life. Mainly it is found in alumni
reminiscence and in college fiction of the nineteenth
century. This does not mean that college life of
to-day lacks human interest. It has that to a far
richer and deeper degree than in its period of
juvenile brigandage. It lacks the jaunty air of
romance in the same way that democracy lacks it;
but it has beneath its somewhat gray and commonplace surface the quick currents of courage and
sacrifice and adventure running full and strong.
The point is not whether the men who wait on the
table at the college commons, or tend furnaces, or
cut wood and do similar unpicturesque jobs are any
better men than the men who painted Professor
Mitchell's horse (in the days of Professor Mitchell
and of horses), or the men who put the cow in the
belfry, or stole Doctor Ball's turkey. Nor is it

[1] From "The President's Report" in the *University Record*,
December, 1916.

whether these of the present generation will make bigger men. The point is simply that student life has undergone a remarkable change, and that the typical college student of to-day is a different sort of person in his college conduct from the student of an earlier generation, and in his attitude toward college life. College life has become more open, and less protected and less privileged, and much more like life on the outside. The sort of ethics that permitted good men in college to do what good men outside never did has been practically discarded; while that fine (and occasionally Quixotic) honor that forbade any college student to do what some acceptable citizens outside constantly do is fortunately preserved.

College men have not yet become too good for the rough uses of this world, but they have made rapid progress in the development of a normal, healthy, responsible, and, at the same time, happy manhood. These new standards of college life and conduct have brought about this important result in the administration of the college: punitive discipline for deliberate misconduct practically does not exist. This fact means, in addition to whatever good results may be inferred from it in student work, that a tremendous amount of time is saved for college administrators who ought to be able to devote their energy to more profitable tasks. With advancing student standards, there has been a steady readjustment of the center of the administrative control of student conduct. Self-government has more fully come to itself, and, like self-support, has passed the self-conscious stage. Affirmative policies of government (to put it briefly) have taken the place of negative policies; faculties have learned that the standards of students are high, and that what is needed is confident and competent leadership, rather than fearsome prodding.

There are times when such a policy would be folly. Perhaps at all times it has an element of danger. Every big human policy is dangerous, for the reason that it is a human and not a mechanical policy. The test is whether it works. Whether it works depends on a number of things, one of the most important being the nature of the material it works with.

Last year, on the recommendation of Dean Stacy, the faculty abolished here the system of "grats." By this so-called system a man was allowed to miss three recitations in the course of a month. If he had over three, he was put on probation. In place of this rule was put the simple statement: "Students are expected to attend all duties." No penalty for failure to meet this expectation was provided, and it was assumed that none would be needed if the students felt that the college seriously regarded class attendance as a personal obligation, and not as a matter of rules. Perhaps it may be felt that there is no difference except in favor of the greater definiteness of the "grat" rule. There is a real difference, however, in attitude, and the essential question is whether this attitude can be, as students say, "put across." Absence records for October and November of this year, the only two full months of completed record, show less than one absence per student per month from any duty. The average number of class duties per student per month is about seventy-five.

I venture to say that the men in college in the country at large are the most serious, the most steady, and the most easily controlled men of their age to be found.

If this appears too good (or too uninteresting) to be readily believed, it may be stated that in addition to full schedules of college duties, students of the University of North Carolina have for the past ten years kept up throughout the winter from seven to ten Sunday schools, covering a radius of six miles from Chapel Hill; that last fall they taught six moonlight schools with 300 pupils enrolled; that they have largely supported for the last six years one of the most influential young missionaries in China—a former student; and that they regularly conduct Sunday schools, night schools, and a Y. M. C. A. for the negroes. During this fall they have run a free lecture lyceum for seven churches and schools in the country around, furnishing twenty-five lecture entertainments to audiences numbering 1,040. All of this they finance and do wholly of their own initiative.

There is no thought of claiming that this work and these students are extraordinary. On the contrary, what I observe here I take to be characteristic of similar institutions throughout the country. I record these observations to emphasize my belief that the North Carolina college student that the educational awakening of fifteen and twenty years ago has called into being in rapidly increasing numbers, is easily the most promising and productive material of all our natural resources.

THE FACULTY[1]

THE center of all these University activities is the University faculty. The faculty is the creating and continuing source of all that has real value in the institution's work. This fact is obvious and commonplace enough, but it is necessary to repeat it and reëmphasize it as long as the habit persists of thinking that what gives distinction to college education is that the place where it is given is called a college. The differences that exist in the quality of the service that colleges render and in their real success are as varied as the differences in any form of business or other organized human enterprise. No divinity hedges about a faculty, exempting it from the normal laws of growth and decay. The group of persons that compose it is unfortunately so merged and leveled by standardization as to somewhat lose individuality from the outside point of view; but the faculty group is made up of nothing but individuals, each unit a positive or negative factor in the sum of the institution's whole present worth: its genius for inves-

[1] From "The President's Report" in the *University Record*, December, 1916.

tigation, its power to teach and to impregnate
youth with the passion for truth and the methods
of truth-seeking—in a word, for that service that
is the soul of progress in a democracy.

The proportion of those individuals in the
faculty who are real persons—who are able, ener-
getic, productive human beings—to those who
are not, determines whether the institution has the
fruitful, growing life of leadership that it ought to
have, or whether it is mediocre and barren, spelling
out its task as a stenciled imitation, merely, of
institutions that vitally count in the work of the
world.

If it is a fact that the faculty is the heart of an
institution's life, it is then the unpardonable sin of
university administration to fail to accept certain
practical responsibilities that necessarily follow it.

The first responsibility rests upon the faculty
itself: the necessity for each person in the faculty
to produce work of distinctive quality in some
legitimate field of university endeavor.

As a whole, our faculty, I confidently believe,
gives evidence in the work it has done and is doing
that it realizes this responsibility. It has worthy
representation in State and national public-service
activities, and has had extraordinary recognition
in national scientific societies. . . .

The second practical responsibility that follows
from the fact that the faculty is the heart of the
institution's life rests upon the Trustees, acting in

behalf of the State: to see to it that the college gets
and keeps the best possible men, that it cultivates
the best in its younger men, and that it surrounds
all of those individuals who compose the faculty
group with conditions that keep the best men at
their best.   This means that no man should be
advanced without a clear affirmative reason that
distinguishes his worth in some important particular from the level of the thousands who crowd
the teaching profession; and it also means that if a
man's work is distinctive he must be justly appreciated and certainly rewarded.   For a college to
earn a proper return on its investment, it must set
as its highest obligation this task of maintaining
such conditions as keep the best men at their best.

The most concise summary of these conditions is
freedom.   For the first thing, freedom from any restraint in reasonable thought and action.   In this
respect our State and Trustees have acted with
great wisdom, and their course has been in every
way splendidly justified.

The faculty should also have freedom from an
excessive mass of routine work.   This is a question
of whether the number of students, and consequently the amount of teaching and outside duties,
is so excessive as to deaden a man's initiative and
productive vitality.   It means simply that the
number of faculty members should increase with
the number of students. . . .

The condition of freedom for productive results

means also freedom from the worry incident to a salary scale too low to admit of reasonably comfortable living. Our salary scale for our best men has always been recognized as too low; but with the rapid increase in the cost of living, and with the advance in faculty salaries elsewhere, it becomes absolutely necessary that some adjustment be made between the quality of the service rendered and the return received. Good men not only cannot do their best work when they are harassed by unpaid bills; but they cannot stay and work with us at all. Competition with other institutions, all other questions aside, requires us to face the fact that real persons of power are worth what they cost—in education even as in business or in the other professions, and that in the long run an institution makes clear what it thinks good men are worth by what it pays them.

I do not mean that the place where teachers will work, or that the quality of the work they do, is determined absolutely by what they get. The record of our faculty makes it clear that such a statement would be grossly untrue. Nor do I mean that no State should ever take a good man from North Carolina. It is the duty of North Carolina to contribute its share of good men to larger fields of service in the nation, just as it is her duty to make due contributions of knowledge to that common stock of knowledge on which she freely draws. We rejoice that we have made our

12

contribution of good men to other sections and to
the nation, and we trust that we shall always continue to do so.   But it is painfully clear that we
have lost more than our share, and lost some of
them simply because other States valued them and
their service far more highly.   If we review the
names of the men that we have lost in the past ten
years, I believe that there will be emphatic agreement that no State in the Union is rich enough in
men nor poor enough in means to have let them go.
To have let them go was a form of stupid extrava-
gance that no organization other than a public
educational enterprise would find it necessary to
commit.

THE SINGLE SUPREME ISSUE[1]

IF North Carolina needs and wants greatly to extend and deepen its educational activities, there is no issue of poverty involved. North Carolina is sufficiently prosperous. It is spending money for what it wants. During 1915 it spent more for the upkeep of automobiles than for the salaries of public school superintendents and teachers combined.

North Carolina has just as much money to spend for education as it wants to spend for education. But even if it were not prosperous, poverty is not an excuse from but a reason for education. What John Owen said in 1830 is as tragically true to-day as then: "It is a policy that has kept the State in ignorance and the poor in poverty."

Let us have done forever with this fatally inverted logic. What we spend is a question of our preference in terms of our wise or unwise choice, and the inevitable index to our desires. A Christian may as well say that the Church is too poor to be honest as for a citizen of North Carolina to

[1] From "The President's Report" in the *University Record*, December, 1916.

say that the State is too poor to educate, and to the limit of its desire.

There is no other issue in North Carolina public policy to-day but this fundamental issue of education. The permanent names in North Carolina statesmanship are those of men who put not words alone but their lives behind the great steps in our educational progress. This is plainly because the fundamentals of democracy have all of their vital roots in education. Equality of opportunity is there, and there alone. To talk of equality of opportunity in circumstances that now exist in our Southern States is political cant.

Our own situation is well known. If we were not callous to it by repetition, if we truly saw it, and keenly sensed the fact that in the full and free education of our people lies the whole secret of progress for which our State exists, we would courageously declare now and make effective a policy that would startle the nation, and make this section what by right it ought to be, the center of the next great forward movement in American progress.

It is an issue more vital to-day than in the days of Murphey, Wiley, Aycock, and McIver. To say in response to such a challenge that the State is too poor is to deny the plain common sense of business and stultify our political faith. It is a mockery of both intelligence and patriotism. Any statesmanship that seeks to evolve a career on any other basis than this necessary basis of education—efficient, unapologetic, complete, abundant—is empty, misleading, and hopelessly barren.

Education is not a local issue. Its standards are relentlessly set in the markets and open forum of the world. A thousand times over we have paid the price for our blindness in the past, and daily for every dollar we saved we now pay tribute ten times over. The immediate future will put us under far greater tribute. The issue is but a new form of the ancient issue of slavery and freedom. An ignorant people are as truly in slavery, economic and intellectual, as if they were in physical bondage. "An educated mind is the genius of democracy. . . . It is the only dictator that freemen acknowledge, and the only security that freemen desire." Without it there is no freedom.

To make actual, vital, and complete through education this ideal that is the common hope and faith of all patriotic North Carolinians is the single-minded mission of the State University. Its relation to the great task is in some respects clear and obvious. It is steadily becoming clearer, both in the radiant light of its past achievements and as it goes about its present pressing and complex work. Different universities, according to the circumstances of their foundation and history, can show different reasons for their existence and for being what they are. But all of them, whatever their date of origin, and whatever their place, have come into being in response to certain needs of their place and time. All of them have been founded with a purpose single in its nature, though diverse in manifestation. That purpose is to make stated and secured provision for the higher needs of a civilized community.

The place of such an institution as a part of the organic life of this State was recognized by its founders, and it was therefore created in the organic law of the State—the first of the state universities. The whole thought of the modern state universities of democracy was afterward outlined by Thomas Jefferson for the State of Virginia, and its foundation regarded by him as an achievement corollary to the authorship of the Declaration of Independence. But neither in North Carolina nor in Virginia could the university exist as a representative democratic institution until the civilization of which it was the expression was truly democratic. That understanding and support of the university came first from the Western States, and from there came a new interpretation of "making stated and secured provision for the higher needs of a civilized community": that it means not merely the needs of the higher and more fortunate classes, but the higher needs of all classes in a civilized community —recognizing in actual fact that the higher needs of all men are identical in direction and equal in impulse.

To catch the true import of that simple and

necessary thought is the supreme achievement of democracy. To realize it as an actuality is to get public ownership of the tools of progress. To understand it is to understand the task of the University.

What it asks, and all that it asks, is not for itself, but as the common instrument of all men concerned in advancing the general welfare and the more abundant life of the State. For this reason it confidently asks, in the first place, for the sympathetic understanding and interest of all those who work with a decent and reasonable regard for the common good, and it asks for such support as will enable it worthily to assist in the solution of the great common problem. If it conceives of its task as one that calls for great equipment, it is not because it is blind to certain limitations, but because it sees beyond limitations to latent powers just as actual and far more real; and finally, and beyond all of this, because it has sure, supreme, and practical faith in the greatness of the State whose representative it is.

THE DECADE AFTER THE WAR[1]

EDUCATIONALLY the decade that follows the war
will be, I believe, the richest and most fruitful in
the nation's history. Here in the South, and in
North Carolina especially, we need to keep heroically foremost in our public policy the determination not to slacken, but rather to quicken our
educational activities during the war. England and
France under war burdens incomparably greater
than ours have doubled their educational budgets.
It is clearly the inevitable policy of wisdom.

Our handling of our educational affairs in the
next few years will furnish once more a test of our
statesmanship and give once more a clear revelation of what relative place we give education in
the things worth while in commonwealth building.
The necessity of war economies will show what we
value in terms of what we nourish and of what we
sacrifice. If schools are the first public-service
institutions closed for lack of fuel; if their terms
are shortened as first steps in economy; if we cease
building them and yet build other things; if they
cannot compete with business for the services of the

[1] From "The President's Report" in the *University Record*,
December, 1917.

few good men and women they need—we shall
know in concrete terms that in time of storm we
feel that they are still the first to be cast overboard,
and not, as we have claimed to believe, the basis
of the democracy for which we are fighting.   No
sacrifice is too great to make for the schools, and
no patriotism is more genuinely productive than
the patriotism whose faith in the schools is so
deeply rooted that no public distraction or disaster
is permitted to blight them as the source of all of
our reconstructive power.

My great confidence in the future of the University is based on the extraordinary need for its
present and future service, and on the spirit of
intelligent sympathy and coöperation that has
been shown by the people in the State at large and
by the faculty, alumni, and students.   The days
ahead of us grow out of the days that are gone;
but in every phase of human activity that a university touches they are new days with a new and
a broader horizon.   They will test the capacity of
the University for leadership, not only in terms of
energy, efficiency, learning, and scholarship, but
in terms of renewed vision, sympathy, and high
devotion.   Out of this new opportunity to serve
in a great and difficult way, and aided, as it wonderfully has been, by the understanding of the State,
whose highest aspiration it seeks to express, I
believe that this institution will come into a new
and especial greatness.

WELCOME TO THE CIVIL WAR CLASSES, 1861–68[1]

FIFTY years ago four hundred gay-hearted boys in answer to the sudden alarm of war left the green shelter of this campus to take up arms in defense of a pleasant land that they loved. To-day in behalf of their Alma Mater, who sent them forth with a mother's benediction, we welcome home their precious remnant with sacred gladness.

When you came here you looked back over fifty years great in the upbuilding of a noble commonwealth; since you left you have lived through fifty years devoted to that same high mission. In the midst of this slow century of fruitful construction are four years of war and desolation, a cataclysm of destruction.

Yet to us who as citizens of an empire that in resurrected strength once more confidently faces the eye of the world, these four blackened and blasted years are the most precious years in all of our history.

[1] An address before the Alumni Association of the University of North Carolina on the occasion of the return at Commencement, 1911, of members of the Civil War Classes to receive their A.B. degrees.

And this is not merely because you left immortal testimony of your bravery on every battlefield of that war; not merely because you widely magnified History's brief catalogue of heroism, and at Manassas, Shiloh, Malvern Hill, Gettysburg, and the rest, gave to Death your beautiful youth as red-handed trophies of your courage; not merely because in all of those tremendous conflicts you crowded loyalty and love into moments of glory, and joyfully stormed at all of "the thousand doors that lead to death."

It is because of the supreme spirit in which you made the supreme sacrifice that is given to men to make. After all of the centuries of civilization, the efforts of learning to teach the selfish conservation of life, the values of self-realization, the sharp calculations that personal ambition makes, there emerges in your example once more the epic paradox: "He that saveth his life shall lose it" and he that loseth his life in great service shall save it. The unforgetting affection of the world is reserved for those who careless of fame and self-aggrandizement have thrown their lives at the foot of a great cause: a Regulus, a Wolfe, a Sidney, a Pettigrew, a Christ; for men who give their lives for a bit of paper, if that paper means freedom; for a murmured prayer, if that prayer means truth; for a flower, if that flower means love; for a trifle of flag, if that flag means home.

The war you waged was as pure a war of service

and ideals as was ever waged by men. It was no war of conquest, nor of vainglory, nor of hate. You loved the Union and you did not fight against her; but you loved your State, and what she stood for, more, and you fought for her with a valor whose radiance unstained by any self-interest becomes more luminous with every passing year.

It is for the spirit in which you made your sacrifice—the love of the man for the land of his birth and the institutions of his fathers, the all-conquering grace of the truly patriotic heart, the eternal verity of "My country, may she ever be right, but right or wrong, my country!"—it is this supreme self-surrender and self-forgetfulness that sanctify all of the temporalities of that war of destruction, and evoke from its terrific annihilations the eternal benediction of peace.

In the nation's holy of holies will still stand your ancient sacrifice, the incarnate patriotism of a continent—History's Calvary becomes its Mount of Transfiguration.

The day on which we welcome you back from your long pilgrimage, then, is more than a festival. For us it is a sacred day. Providence that has graciously prolonged your lives into generations whose highest hope is to emulate your virtues, and so has made you witnesses of your own immortality, is doubly gracious to us in giving to us this new inspiration of your presence. Your Alma Mater that sent you forth a mother of sorrows welcomes you home, a mother of exceeding great joy. To her you are not gray-haired old men, but her own immortal boys, ever young and ever fair. To her the holy twilight of your lives shades not into the darkness of the night; but lightens into the eternal youth and beauty of the stars. For her your great deeds, and the patriotic impulse that glorifies them will ever be an inspiration in her eternal business of making for the service of the State noble-hearted men!

ON BEING INDUCTED INTO THE STU-
DENTS' ARMY TRAINING CORPS[1]

WE are met to-day to re-assert in a spirit of high
and solemn consecration our active faith in the
principles of freedom, justice, and equality, on
which this nation was founded, and out of which
it has grown in beauty and strength to its present
power.

We mean to say here to-day, as our fathers said—
and as the wholesome heroic heart of men will
always say—that there are certain rights of liberty
and life inalienable for men everywhere; and that
whenever the vital growth of these rights is men-
aced we will be quick to defend them as a heritage
more precious than life itself.

We are happy to-day as we accept the sword of
defense of these ancient and eternal principles;
and more for the opportunity of a wider and deeper
interpretation of them, that makes our present
cause the equal cause of the liberal brotherhood of
all good men everywhere, and makes the cause of
our country the common cause of a free mankind.

[1] An Address before the Students of the University of North
Carolina, October 1, 1918.

Is it fanciful to think that the heroes of freedom, whose stories we have studied here—of Thermopylæ, of Runnymede, of Bunker Hill and the rest—give to us, in the beauty of this quiet spot, their benediction, as we take from their hands the torch of the eternal task, and "carry on" to a new and greater victory?

The spirit of this campus, the spirit of our State and our country, the spirit of the world to-day, assure to us the continuing courage and complete devotion that will bring to a glorious fulfillment the noblest adventure that ever called to the aspiring spirit of youth.

GREETINGS FROM THE STATE COLLEGES[1]

ON behalf of the State Colleges, I am happy to bring to Meredith College and to her new President the greetings and felicitations of whole-hearted comradeship, and congratulations as spontaneous and as affectionate as your gracious generosity—and the proprieties of the occasion—will permit you to accept!

With sure confidence, we bid you Godspeed on this day bright with fresh promise of good fortune, and for reasons too obvious for careful searching: for your fidelity to those simple tasks of sound teaching that are the main mission of all of us; for courageously pressing ahead with steady courage to higher standards of scholarship; for the splendid breadth of spirit that has enabled you so finely to interpret your work as a part of a great common cause.

This last is the obvious reason that happily makes this occasion quite as much ours as it is yours. You chance to be here in Raleigh, and to be responsible to the Baptist church, and to be teach-

[1] An Address delivered at the Inauguration of Dr. Charles Edward Brewer as President of Meredith College at Raleigh, N. C., February 3, 1916.

ing young women; while we happen to live in Greensboro, or Boone, or Chapel Hill, and to be responsible to the State at large, and to be teaching men, perhaps. These are merely the variant but converging lines along which we work; for the saving grace (if you will pardon the expression)— the saving grace of all of our work depends on the insight, vigor, and patient sympathy with which, each of us, each in his own place and after his own kind, sees that work as directed toward the common end of the whole, abundant life of the State, and to make that as fully and richly fruitful as may be.

You come to this day of fresh inspiration at a moment singularly rich and wonderful in opportunity to the American college as an institution, and especially so to the Southern college for women. There are many ways in which the college may approach its task; but two ways are fundamental for all of us to master and to reconcile; and, because they are fundamental, I never tire of trying to keep them freshly before me. The college must help a man or a woman to master the art of making a good living—justifying existence by productive labor in God's good world of things; and it must help a man or a woman to master the art of living a complete life—justifying existence in God's great world of ideas and ideals. In neither of these aspects of education has Southern opinion given sufficient emphasis to the education of women.

13

Generally speaking, the public is not concerned about the higher education of women, except for those who mean to teach. The colleges themselves, therefore have, perhaps, not felt able to apply themselves with the high seriousness that the task demanded.

And yet, the home, if I may put the matter in an unqualified word or two, is the clearing house of our whole material and spiritual income and expenditure. In ninety per cent., I venture to say, of the homes that the students of this college will preside over, the woman in the partnership will spend necessarily over sixty per cent. of the total income. In the great economy of making a good living, she is quite as important as the man. Our education has not taken sufficient account of this simple fact. We have said with some unction that "woman's place is in the home"—which is at once both a wise, beautiful, and also a very stupid thing to say, unless we realize the fact that the home, and the office, and the store, and the farm are an organic union in the economy of living. The college for women needs to take intelligent account of woman's relation to this great business, and it needs to help her interpret it in terms of large and liberal efficiency. Otherwise it fails.

But the college also fails, and fails tragically, if it does no more than train its students to be efficient in the task of doing a necessary job well, and even accumulating material wealth. Material efficiency would find the means to shape men and women to its sharp and narrow necessities even if liberal colleges did not exist. Indeed the thought now and then assails us that material efficiency and the passion to "get on" in the world of things is already making it so that the liberal arts college cannot exist. But this is a passing phase, and it is still the great function of the college to fix above the essential of making the means to live the supreme necessity of creating the true wealth of life. "There is," as Ruskin says, "no wealth but Life, —Life, including all of its powers of love and joy and of admiration." The curriculum of the college represents still the whole treasury of the human race—and it is the unique and sacred privilege of colleges to preserve to mankind through a period when practical efficiency and general material welfare are compelling attention away from certain aspects of culture, to maintain at every hazard the standards of sound scholarship, of learning, of beauty, of truth made visible in daily affairs, and to translate the temporary appetites of hand to mouth existence into the durable satisfactions of life.

Here is the opportunity of the college, if it can vitally comprehend it; and to the Southern college for women it is once more an opportunity singularly rich and wonderful, for here again public opinion has not taken it as seriously as it should, nor equipped it as adequately as it should for its task.

If our civilization is ever to be what all good men wish it to be, it will be so not through the identity of the function of men and women in doing the work of the world; but through equal opportunity to enjoy and freely exercise their human aspirations for fuller knowledge, keener appreciation, wider and richer service.   And because I believe in the equal humanity of women, I believe in equal privileges to them in the humanities, and in their superior opportunity to saturate our life with the curative and liberating influences of the humanities.   I do not believe that the sweetness and light of womanhood is necessarily made garish by the sweetness and light of the culture of the race.   One may pay homage to a gracious and charming woman, and at the same time pay homage to a more complete womanhood, a greater *humanhood*. I believe, therefore, that the standards of scholarship of the college for women should be as high as those of the college for men; its faculty as well paid and strong; its laboratories as well equipped; its mental demands and mental discipline as severe, its intent as definite and full of conviction.   Such parts of its present curriculum as cannot be interpreted in these terms of creating the ultimate wealth of life should be discarded; but whatever parts may be, should be administered with the sincerity, passion, and power of the eternal verities.

You will understand, Mr. President, that I am not trying to give you advice.   You, no doubt, understand these things far better than I. I am trying to emphasize the fact that your colleagues in that part of our joint faculty, known as the State colleges, though separated from you by greater or less distance, would have you steadily know that we appreciate both the dignity and the difficulty of your task, and we greet you to-day, not under the impulse of a momentary surge of friendliness, preliminary to a relapse into unsympathetic competition; we greet you as our colleague and we come to do unaffected honor to you to-day, and to pledge to you, through length of days, the coöperation, understanding, and loyal support of men and women who pray that no personal or partial good may obscure the highest good for which we all labor, and without which all our labor is vain. We say this in no perfunctory way, but as our deepest conviction, which we know we must realize in practice before our educational life can be liberated in its full power. We shall rejoice with you in the great days of achievement ahead of you, and we shall sympathize with you in discouragements not less certain to come—and "our hearts in strength of brother's welcome," welcome you to the full strength and inspiration that will come from both!

IV

Occasional Papers

THE POETRY OF JOHN CHARLES McNEILL[1]

FOR the first time in the history of North Carolina there is a conscious effort toward the production of literature of sufficient force and volume to be taken account of as a movement. Men of power, for the first time, are expressing themselves with confidence in the written rather than the spoken word, and in the fields of scholarship and literature are producing work that in aspiration at least competes with work in the world market of the best thoughts and feelings. At last we have a group of writers. In the past two years native North Carolinians have produced in North Carolina in critical biography, in philology, in history and in historical criticism, in political and social science, in general science, in literary criticism, in prose essays, and in poetry, incomparably better work than at any other period of our history. During this minute period the aggregate in these lines of endeavor surpasses in general appeal the accumulated product of our entire previous history. In a sense we have just begun to produce

[1] From the *South Atlantic Quarterly*, January, 1907.

books, and beginnings challenge notice and analysis.

Mr. John Charles McNeill, first to be honored among this group of writers by the presentation of the Patterson Cup, is the first North Carolina poet to win the ear of the whole State. As a newspaper worker he is the immediate successor of the only writer who has made a successful appeal to the State through a volume of prose, the right of which to exist is based upon what may be loosely called its literary qualities. Avery's *Idle Comments* and Mr. McNeill's *Songs Merry and Sad* are not a part of a spent movement; conditions fortify the hope that they are pioneers. North Carolina has now a reading public that may be safely relied upon as permanent.

These *Songs Merry and Sad* with confidence may be put with the half dozen slender volumes that make up the achievement of the State in verse. In many respects it is the most poetic collection by a North Carolinian that has yet appeared. Boner's *Lyrics* alone competes with it for the first place; and the provincial point of view at once suggests that the greater part of these *Lyrics* was composed in the long while that the author was a part of, and under the literary influences of, the literary life of New York City. Boner, like Poe, lost the curious fascination of locale. The provincial point of view sacrifices no regrets over the present poet. He is a part of the local group, and he represents vividly—just as Avery did in prose—the essence of local fine feeling.

Not that he is to be damned with the paradoxical epithet, "a local poet." He is not even what is called "Southern" in his mood; and he is among the few poets born south of the line that has marked literary limitations, not less heavily than political, who have not surrendered their inspiration wholly to the tyranny of Poe, Lanier, and Timrod. He has none of the offended melancholy that, though it may not be characteristic of the best poets of the South, is characteristic of Southern verse. No boding owls or humid moons haunt his verse, but there is the calm, flute-like note of the wood thrush and the mood of "silver silence,"

And cottage crofts where apples bend the bough,

luring the tired heart into comfortable peace.

He is of a place very definitely, but he is not provincial. The place is home, and he revives it with all of its rich connotations. Hearthstone moods, and the little loves and sorrows are his theme,

The little cares and carols that belong
    To home-hearts and old mystic lutes and lyres,
    And spreading acres, where calm-eyed desires
Wake with the dawn, unfevered, fair and strong.

These he voices in a varied and adequate verse medium, in felicitous and always unpretentious diction, and with a sympathy that within its range lacks nothing of nobility.

It is his intuitive sympathy that dominates. His verse is melodious with full-toned, deeply breathed sympathy. For the little white bride, the invalid, the baby in its crib, the drudge, the caged bird, the prisoner, the mother, the wife, and for her who is a mother but not a wife, it is the same: the love that understands without the need of formalism or creed. With subjects saturated with sentiment he appears to have no temptation to sentimentality. The reserve of sincerity holds the balance perfectly true. It is his spontaneous sympathy, however, that takes the emphasis. Reserve is a characteristic of almost all present verse, but present verse has lost interest in those simple fundamental tones and moods that it has been the peculiar function of poetry best to express. Exquisite technique our poets have, and startling insight, and an immense curiosity in the hidden things. Emotion has given over its place to the subtleties of introspection and super-suggestion. At a time when poetry has lost the appeal of passion, it is peculiarly grateful to come into the warm confidence of emotion always gentle, intimate, and manly, and in its best moments, infinitely tender. It is a rare and blessed thing when Great Heart is given the gift of speech.

The love poems exhibit the highest pitch of Mr.

McNeill's singing quality. Quite frankly with him love is the one thing worth while. The tender depth of *Love's Fashion*, *Now*, and *Pardon Time*, the graceful spontaneity of *Jane's Birthday*, and the passionate abandon of *Oh Ask Me Not*, show his power to portray with subtlety and flexibility strong, sweet passion.

The sincerity and the naturalness of the elemental sympathy expressed in this collection suggest Burns. Perhaps most obviously because we know that the author is Scotch. His inspiration, however, follows the larger line of Scotch impulse rather than that of Burns. Scotchmen are the best expression of ingleside moods. Mr. McNeill does not show any influence of Burns, just as he does not show any influence of Southern poets, he has no apparent "master"; but he carries out the traditions of Scotch poetry not only in the sympathetic presentation of home, but—and here Scotch poetry has made its great contribution to English literature—the steadfast love of simple aspects of Nature. For this last Mr. McNeill suggests Wordsworth, too. He has immensely less of insight, of course, because lacking the religious fervor of Wordsworth's contemplation of nature, he never gets free from fleshly suggestion; but because of the good fleshly suggestion he has a more appealing human sweetness. The simplicity of his presentation also suggests Wordsworth. *The Secret* is notably successful for its incisive

simplicity, with its "wind and flower and pale
moonbeam"—where

> A wind, as wandering winds will do,
>> Brought to the baby there
> Sweet smells from some quaint flower that grew
>> Out on some hill somewhere.

He does not pursue simplicity with the zeal of an
apostle, however, and in the lines quoted above
comes nearest to achieving the finality of self-
effacement where "Nature seems to take the pen
and write."

Just as his sympathy is spontaneous and not the
result of modern altruism, so his representation of
Nature is not a part of the back to Nature movement. Nature with him is not an acquired taste.
To say it tritely he is a lover of Nature rather than
a student of Nature. His knowledge has come by
absorption rather than by analysis, by association
rather than by reflection. At least one gets these
impressions from reading his verse. He doesn't
patronize Nature by an appearance of pride in
knowing little facts about her. A primrose by the
river's brim remains a yellow primrose in his verse,
but he reveals again that a simple primrose may
be so much! The mere naming of it may suggest
all of the beauty that is its excuse for being, and
revive the swift, elusive joy that

> quivers in the bliss
> Where roses blow. . . .

In nature poetry lack of reflection of course does not mean lack of revelation. To say that the treatment is obvious does not mean that it is not as profound as any. *Songs Merry and Sad* interpret Nature by presenting her simple aspects only with eye and ear responsive to each sensitive shade of meaning. *October* and *September* reveal real power to discriminate landscapes, and to revive in fullness and beauty landscape moods.

Affectionate observation of Nature is apt to lead imperceptibly from the most obvious things to the most profound. "The mysterious powers themselves that men call God that move and live and have their will behind the blowing wind, and the rising sap, behind the drifting leaf and the granite hills. . . " these mysterious powers, in poetry, in the naming of the wind, the sap, the drifting leaf and the granite hills, move and live and have their will once more. It is so in the present collection; there is not much deliberately expressed philosophy.

> Hill wrapped in gray, standing along the west;
>   Clouds dimly lighted gathering slowly;
> The star of peace at watch above the crest—
>   Oh, holy, holy, holy!

This is the heart of its philosophy. Contemplation of Nature shades off into worshipful quiescence rather than rises into ecstasy. Mr. McNeill is not disturbed by the beautiful mystery that he sees

about him, though he sees the beauty and is conscious of the mystery. It arouses in him no anxious question and excites no fever of curiosity.
He is content to sit

> Between the tents of hope and sweet
>   Rememberings.

In the end love will have its righteous way in
peace. *Vision*, *L'Envoi*, *The Invalid*, and *The
Christman Hymn* all express variations on this
mood.

When merry milkmaids to their cattle call
    At evenfall
    And voices range
Loud through the gloam from grange to quiet grange,

Wild waif-songs from long distant lands and loves,
    Like migrant doves,
    Wake and give wing
To passion dust-dumb lips were wont to sing.

The new still holds the old moon in her arms;
    The ancient charms
    Of dew and dusk
Still lure her nomad odors from the musk,

And at each day's millennial eclipse,
    On new men's lips,
    Some old song starts,
Made of the music of millennial hearts,

Whereto one listens as from long ago
    And learns to know
    That one day's tears
And love and life are as a thousand years,

And that some simple shepherd, singing of
    His pain and love
    May haply find
His heart-song speaks the heart of all his kind.

This *Folk Song* expresses something of the mood
and function of *Songs Merry and Sad*. It is a
collection deeply sympathetic and true, with real
sweetness and with inspiration equally real and
true. Conviction of great poetic power we seldom
feel in reading it, but the presence of the divine
gift of poetry we are always sensible of—the gift
to minister to some need of the spirit—as when a
simple heart-song speaks the heart of all mankind.

14

A NORTH CAROLINA TEACHER[1]

To men in every profession now and then come doubts as to the real productiveness of their work. Prof. Barrett Wendell said (or is reported to have said) sometime ago to a promising student that he should avoid the profession of teaching because "it is a sterile field." One virtue at least distinguishes this judgment of Professor Wendell's: It frankly avoids the cant that so often marks the talk about teaching and other noble and (consequently) poorly paid professions. A North Carolina teacher several years ago raised a small storm in the State by a judgment similar in frankness: that the teachers in the State need not be indignant at their small wages—that most of them got as much as they are worth. To judge a man's worth is often very difficult. In business it is fairly easy; in medicine it is somewhat more difficult; in teaching it is more difficult still. Effects there are not so quickly and obviously related to their causes. If it were possible to inoculate a man with the binomial theorem and Browning and have him break out the next day or the next week

[1] From the *North Carolina Review*, February 5, 1911.

with dollar bills or a case of bankruptcy, judgment would be easy. And for better and worse teachers would get more accurately what they are worth. Straight-thinking teachers do well to find and to speak the naked truth about their profession, but he is a sadly astray guide who calls teaching "a sterile field." That will not be true until pliable humanity is worn down to a breed of barren metal. Experience reveals a different display of facts. Few of the achievements of men have been solitary triumphs. They were first laid with words of grateful discipleship at the feet of some teacher.

The sterility of a field depends as much on the husbandman as it does on the field, and a greater variety of conditions surrounds the fruitful cultivation of men than surrounds the successful cultivation of the soil. The productiveness of teaching in Massachusetts may not be as obvious, though it may be just as real as it is in North Carolina; it may not be as obvious in the work of one teacher in Harvard as it is in that of another. Professor George H. Palmer, for instance, a colleague of Professor Wendell's, has said that if for any reason Harvard College could not pay him for teaching he would gladly pay Harvard College for letting him teach. This confession wakes a clear echo in the heart of every true teacher, and bears with it stimulating assurance of productiveness. The experience of Dr. Thomas Hume, Professor Emeritus of English Literature in the University of North

Carolina, is an illuminating example of the somewhat puzzling rewards of the profession of teaching.
For him all active work is done. At its finish he
finds himself with no accumulation of wealth, nor
other visible accumulation. His influence is not
apparent from a casual glance at present educational work. Shall one say, then, that teaching
was to him "a sterile field?"

In 1885, when Dr. Hume came to the University,
conditions surrounding teaching in the State were
not so favorable as they are now. They were especially unfavorable to the teaching of English
Literature. The State was to wait five years for
the great educational campaign of the '90's. Mc-
Iver was at that time a teacher of English in Peace
Institute; Alderman had just begun his public
school work in Goldsboro; Joyner was a teacher
in the Winston schools; Aycock's educational
activity was entirely local.

And even when this awakening movement was
underway the impetus of its enthusiasm was
necessarily along fundamental lines. It was for a
wider intelligence and a higher intelligence among
the people. Its message was primarily a message of
efficiency. Its compelling word was to men as
workers. It said to agriculture and commerce—
your fight will end in tragic defeat unless you can
use your head as well as your hands. To know in
order to do was its winning battle cry. It put enthusiasm into many branches of learning, but it

put less into literature than into any of the rest. Literature, as such, has nothing to say on this matter of the utility of knowledge. It deals with fine feeling rather than effective knowing, and views men not merely as capable of doing successful work, but as capable of enjoying the noblest emotions. In the face of the difficulties that confront every teacher of the æsthetic, and the peculiar difficulties that confronted him, Dr. Hume wrought at his task of teaching the masterpieces of literature with the zeal of a prophet. Literature (whenever he wrote the word he capitalized it) was to him not a chance profession; it was a religious faith. The beauty he found there was not the sentimentalism of a cult; it was the gift of God, co-equal with truth and with goodness—the heavenly light that was the consecration of the monotonous struggle to get on. The prophetic earnestness with which he revealed his vision made him not a little absurd (a sure effect of greatly earnest men) to many of the absurd youths he taught; but under all discouragements he never faltered in his faith, and not one youth, however absurd, failed to take out into his life something of the divine fire that inspired Dr. Hume.

During most of the sixteen years in which he served the State, Dr. Hume in his field worked almost alone. Alone in what was by all odds the largest department in the University he placed but one limit on the number of courses he taught and that was the number of hours in the day. Day and night he gave himself to active instruction. In addition, he organized Shakespeare clubs out in the State, lectured in summer schools, preached in churches, in fact, put no reserve whatever upon his time or his strength. It was a matter of everyday wonder how so frail a man had the burden-bearing power of a superman. But here was the simple secret: To him it was not a burden, but a joy. It gave him the chance to teach! And now that weakness remorselessly holds him to his room, when the long, long thoughts that are the heritage of age as well as the promise of youth come to him, I question if thought of gratitude on the part of the State for the strength spent in her service ever crosses his mind. Gratitude to the State, on the contrary, no doubt he feels that he was given worthy work to do—that gracious benediction of a fruitful life no doubt he feels and nothing more.

Besides the influence that Dr. Hume exerted on all of his students, on the thousands of people with whom he came in contact in his extension work and through his preaching, he made other leaders of sweetness and light in whose work his influence is especially obvious. Many successful teachers, themselves makers of teachers, many successful preachers and lawyers have added a grace to their lives that was kindled at the torch that he bore. He was never a writer of books, but he was a maker of writers of books.

From a material viewpoint, teaching has been to him "a sterile field"; but the fine thing is that he stands quite clearly and unconsciously above the material viewpoint. The cessation of work does not mark the end of his influence, nor do the four walls of his room limit its sphere. As a teacher of men it was given to him to subdue the petty tyranny of time and space. Is it not possible to say simply and with certitude about such a teacher that life gives to him her greatest gift: that even while he lives immortality becomes to him a visible, a realized fact?

The stream which overflowed the soul was passed away,
A consciousness remained that it had left
Deposited upon the silent shore
Of memory images and precious thoughts
That shall not die, and cannot be destroyed.

THE ESSAYS OF SAMUEL McCHORD CROTHERS[1]

THE appearance of a third volume of essays by Dr. Crothers is a pleasurable rather than a significant event. It wrestles with no bristling, new doctrines, teaches no psychic attitudes, and does not assert any right to a place among the "books that have helped" somebody. Along with *The Gentle Reader*, and *The Pardoner's Wallet*, *The Christmas Fire* will unobtrusively find a place in that Standard Library of Pleasant Books that someone has suggested will one day delight the world in a uniform collection.

Admission into this library will not be determined wholly by content. Lamb will be welcomed, but Carlyle must stay out, and Lamb will be welcomed partly for the very reason that Carlyle would kick him out of the conventional standard library. He lacked the harrowing "somewhat" mood that Carlyle declared always essential. "His speech has not an opinion in it, or a fact," said Carlyle, "that you can thank him for." ("A more pitiful, rickety . . . Tom-fool I do not know," he also said.)

[1] From the *South Atlantic Quarterly*, April, 1909.

But perhaps this mood of high seriousness has been rather over-assertive in English literature. Criticism of life is understood in a too strictly pedagogical sense,

> a rod
> To check the erring and reprove.

High seriousness is all well enough in its way, but it is precisely the mood that one does not find in some of what are most assuredly the best parts of Chaucer and Shakespeare, and in Izaak Walton and Goldsmith—God rest their genial souls in peace!— and in a hundred others, who not only had the gift of wisdom, but the final gift of graciously imparting it. Pleasantness is not to be always patronized as "mere pleasantness." It, too, has its universal values. "We have the right to ask of our poets to be pleasant companions when they discourse on the highest themes." Let youth struggle up difficult steeps with its banners of strange device, and let reformers glorify their grimy fight in "the smoke and stir of this dim spot"; there are those that like their literature that way, and it is a good way, but let them not talk down to the Standard Library of Pleasant Books. Let them remember that serenity has always been a characteristic of the countenance of truth. It is just this mood in her, that Solomon, in his succinct comments on wisdom, emphasizes: "Her ways are ways of pleasantness, and all her paths are peace."

It is important that Dr. Crothers has wise things to say, but it is more important that he says them in the ways of pleasantness. His essays are criticisms of life; but their chief contribution is not their content, it is their illuminating and interpreting point of view. The titles of the volumes are fairly suggestive of what this is.

Mr. Crothers is first of all "a gentle reader," and a considerable portion of his essays is devoted to pleasant talk about books and reading. In his first book he discusses among other topics: The Gentle Reader, The Enjoyment of Poetry, The Mission of Humor, That History Should be Readable, Some Honorable Points of Ignorance and Quixotism. All of these he converses about in the spirit of gentle culture that marks the old-fashioned bookman of plates and stalls. In his second volume he talks about life rather than books, and treats of "aspects of human nature which, while open to friendly criticism, are excusable." He is the gentle reader still—a "gentle reader" is no variable!—but he is more directly the critic of his fellows, and assumes the garb of a sort of idealized Pardoner, with such themes as The Unseasonable Virtues, Prejudices, The Cruelty of Good People. The third volume is smaller than either of the others, containing three essays on Christmas, one on Being a Doctrinaire, and one on The Ignominy of Being Grown Up. The spirit is the same whether he is talking of books or of people, a spirit of large and sympathetic leisure, of spiritual mellowness and fruitfulness.

Such a manner does not lend itself to quotation. One cannot quote a mood. The atmosphere of the gentle reader's library is not a subject for analysis by sample. The air is tempered to a comfortable warmth, that is enough; and, drop in when you will, an agreeable companion and a stimulating conversation await you.

"The nature of each individual," says Dr. Crothers, "has its point of moral saturation. When this point is reached, it is of no use to continue exhortation or rebuke on any kind of didactic effort. Even the finest quality of righteous indignation will no longer soak in. With me the point of moral saturation comes when I attend more meetings of a reformatory and denunciatory character than nature intended me to profit by. If they are well distributed in point of time, I can take in a considerable number of good causes and earnestly reprobate an equal number of crying evils. But there is a certain monotony of rebuke which I am sure is not beneficial to persons of my disposition. That some things are wrong I admit, but when I am peremptorily ordered to believe that everything is wrong, it arouses in me a certain obstinacy of contradiction. I might be led to such a belief, but I will not be driven to it. I rebel against those censors of manners and morals who treat all human imperfectness with equal rigor.

To relax even for an instant the righteous frown over the things that are going wrong, into an indulgent smile at the things that are not nearly so bad as they seem, is in their eyes nothing less than compounding a felony. If they allow proper intervals between protests so that the conscience could cool down, all would be well. But this is just what they will not allow. The wheels must go round without intermission until progress is stopped by the disagreeable accident of 'a hot box.'

"You remember, after Mrs. Proudie had given her guests a severe lesson in social ethics, the Signora asked in her hearing,—

"'Is she always like this?'

"'Yes—always, madam,' said Mrs. Proudie, returning, 'always the same—always equally adverse to impropriety of conduct of every description.'

"Mrs. Proudie was an excellent woman according to her light, yet Barchester would have been a happier place to live in had her light been less constant. A little flicker now and then, a momentary relief from the glare, would have been appreciated."

Dr. Crothers has an essay on "The Mission of Humor" that is a continuous illustration of humor, although in it he does not tell a joke. He is too genuine a humorist for that. "Ostentatious jocosity," he says, is not to his liking. Humor with him is not a crackling jest, it is a profoundly pleasant and illuminating way of looking at life.

Erasmus, he notes, described a sort of humor the characteristics of which are good temper, insight into human nature, a certain reserve, and a gentle irony that makes the praise of folly not unpleasing to the wise. This grateful sort of humor Dr. Crothers has, and not the fantastic whimsies that are the by-products of seriousness. He has not the full freighted weight of opinion that one meets in the essays of Mr. A. C. Benson, nor the crisp modernity of Mr. E. S. Martin, nor the restless brilliancy of the paradoxical Mr. Chesterton. His richly genial temper is as unique in the present essay as the similar temper of Mr. William De Morgan is in present fiction.

Contemporary essayists make epigrammatic glitter a leading characteristic of their form, and the conception is not wholly contemporary. De Quincey affirms: "An essayist should make every sentence sparkle. . . . The narrow limit within which the essayist works demands superior merit in the performance." Superior merit meant to him intellectual artistry. But there is—at least with some of the best of present essayists—an irritating monotony of verbal brilliance. Frosted globes would better serve the purposes of illumination; one asks for a little more sweetness and a little less light. Paradoxes cease to stimulate the nervous organism,—Chestertonics leave us after a while dull and listless, and we gratefully fall back upon the herb called heartsease.

This is as much as to say that we seek the healing spirit of literature rather than wit or knowledge. "Literary values," says Dr. Crothers, "inhere not in things or even in ideas, but in persons. There are some rare spirits that have imparted themselves to their words. The book then becomes a person and reading comes to be a kind of conversation. The reader is not passive, as if he were listening to a lecture on The Ethics of the Babylonians, he is sitting by his fireside and old friends drop in on him." Where literary values really inhere it is a difficult matter to say, but the portion of literature that all lovers of books hold most dear is that made up of the books that have become persons. The essays of Dr. Crothers belong to this class. The dominating mood is their essential friendliness, and the person is the right sort! He has the delicacy of feeling, the charm of manner, the gentle culture, the kindly communicative warmth that make our friends and our books our only intimate delights.

THE READING OF CHILDREN [1]

MR. JOHN JAY CHAPMAN expresses in a recent essay the opinion that the most important part of our education consists of what we had read to us before we could read. However this may be, the matter of the reading of children has had in recent years rapidly increasing attention on the part of educators and publishers. As the child has been taken more seriously, and treated with more dignity, the reading provided for him has lost the sweet insipidity that it had fifteen years ago. Children's books that are good may be had now at any price one chooses to pay. One cheap collection that is good is that found in the juvenile section of "Everyman's Library," published by Dutton & Co., New York. The price is low, and the mechanical make-up is in every respect good. A more expensive collection is the complete library for children published by Houghton, Mifflin & Co.

Everybody who cares for good books should know of this admirable "Everyman's Library." It answers well both of those inevitable questions: "What can I read," and "Where can I get it." The sensation created by the "Five Foot Shelf"

[1] From the *North Carolina Review*, August 7, 1910.

was due in large measure to the belief that it satisfied the common desire to get at the best books with the least trouble. Subscription agents are able to make their enormous profits from the simple fact of their bringing the man in direct contact with the book. The list of books published in this "Everyman's Library" contains now over four hundred and fifty standard titles. Merely to read over the list is to make a valuable point of contact with the best books.

To have undertaken the publication of these books at so low a figure is a contribution to the education and happiness of the race; to have made the venture successful by its liberal patronage of what is good is greatly to the credit of a public whose patronage of what is bad has been a favorite topic of authors since the world began.

Another essayist, as well known as Mr. Chapman, recently ascribed all of the deficiencies of present education to bad choice in the books of children. "They should be turned," he said, "to the classics. They need to be stirred by, and become hero-worshipers of Achilles and Odysseus and Siegfried and King Arthur." So far this is well enough; but after a bitter arraignment of the present age the essayist continues: "They need to live in worlds in which the dollar neither bought nor measured anything worth having." In like manner Mr. Chapman, in the essay previously quoted, finds the case of good reading in so bad a

time altogether pitiable. The case is pretty bad,
but it is not all on one side. There is so much to
be said on the other side that I refrain from saying
anything except this one certain thing: the liber-
ally cultured rail at the age more than is good for
them. Railing isn't the best thing to develop
sweetness and light. It doesn't lead to truth—
doesn't lead anywhere, in fact. There are people,
it seems, who cannot enjoy their literature without
deriding people who enjoy their ledgers. They
delight so keenly in Philistinism in others that they
forget the danger of Pharisaism in themselves.

Better reasons exist for good reading than that
a commercial age doesn't read and is bad. Children, for instance, should read about Achilles, and
Odysseus, and Siegfried, and King Arthur, by all
means; but they should read about them because
they will get deep and abiding joy from this reading and not because these heroes "lived in a world
in which the dollar neither bought nor measured
anything worth having." I doubt if such a world
ever existed. If such a world did exist present
children cannot be wholly absorbed by its standard,
because of the fact that they live in a world in
which the dollar measures a great many things
indubitably worth having.

One of them, by the way, is a good book record-
ing the lives of Siegfried, Arthur, and Odysseus.
They will find there that after Siegfried married Kriemhild they measured much happiness

15

from the dollars stolen from the Nibelungen princes.

The average man who has the ambition to read good books (and almost every average man has) is altogether helpless when the rare moment comes at which he is to begin. He finds a comfortable chair and adjusts it comfortably to the light and to the fire and then—where is the book.

Perhaps he has had willed to him "Lubbock's Hundred Best Books," or perhaps he has bought Dr. Eliot's "Five Foot Shelf." He doesn't know, even after this much winnowing down where to begin, any more than Dr. Eliot would know where to begin if he should be carried out to St. Louis and told to buy the fall stock for a hardware store. But the average man with the ambition to read must begin somewhere, so he logically begins at one end of his Five Foot Shelf, planning to go straight across. He happens to strike first *The Origin of Species*. It is as hard as nails and he cannot possibly read it. He tries the other end and pulls down *The Divine Comedy*. This he finds as unintelligible as an acre of tangled twine. This average man doesn't tackle the reading problem again for five years.

The trouble is obvious. The particular case failed to find its particular book. The genuine desire to read was there, and the book that would have satisfied the desire was there, but the happy accident that would have brought them together didn't occur.   A shelf of standard books is like a shelf of standard remedies.   It is fundamental and excellent, but a person who doesn't know what he needs can't be sent to it in the dark with any sort of expectation of pleasurable results.   Quite the contrary.

THE GREATNESS OF TWO GREAT MEN[1]

IN a recent magazine essay called "The Devil's Advocate," Professor Brander Matthews vigorously attacks the greatness of Dr. Samuel Johnson, Thomas Carlyle, and John Ruskin. He says that we cannot find out too soon that these men are not "truly entitled to be held aloft." Ruskin he declares is dogmatic and arrogant, and altogether discredited as a critic of art and as a critic of life. Carlyle he charges with a bad style, bad manners, intolerance, envy, and lack of sympathy with democracy and science. Johnson he finds in much the same way, underbred and narrow-minded, without critical worth and with a style of the most evil influence.

Two of these figures that Professor Matthews attacks are very deeply set in the affection of all English-speaking people. Ruskin the great majority are fairly indifferent to. Though they have a definite opinion that he performed a big task with eloquence and courage, he has no such hold on the heart of the race as have the other two. Johnson and Carlyle are fine figures to love, and English-speaking people, whether they read their works or

[1] From the *North Carolina Review*, September 4, 1910.

not, love the memory of them as they love the great characters in their fiction and the heroes in their folklore.

The interesting thing about Professor Matthews's attack is not that as a critic of superior insight he tells us that these supposedly great men are really not great. That in its way is interesting. To pull down an historically great man is even more interesting than the pathetic spectacle of pulling down an historically great building. The vitally interesting thing is that after the critic has finished his work, after he has apparently proved that many things that Johnson and Carlyle said are not true, that the way they say it is inartistic, and that as men they were socially unacceptable, after he says all of this with grace and point, the greatness of the men he attacks is as serenely unbelittled as if the Devil's Advocate had not spoken.

And the reason for this anomaly is not that the people are blindly prejudiced worshipers, wedded to their idols. Professor Matthews attacks the eminence of these great men at a point where their greatness does not lie. What he overlooks, and what many other critics overlook, is that there is an element in the greatness of great men, even in that of literary men, that is deeper than what they say, and deeper than rhetorical analysis of how they say it.

Samuel Johnson is a splendid illustration. Pro-

fessor Matthews says that Johnson is the easiest of
the three for the Devil's Advocate to demolish.
He would be if the basis of Professor Matthews's
criticism were correct. As a matter of fact, Johnson is the most difficult of the three for the Devil's
Advocate to demolish. Horace Walpole said more
forcefully almost precisely what Professor Matthews says about Johnson, and it has all been said
a hundred times in the intervening century. But
the critics are all of a sort. They try to show that
Johnson was not a literary artist, and a literary
artist of the sort that Thomas Gray, for instance,
was. To show that is a very easy matter. There
is more beauty in one stanza that Gray threw out
of his great *Elegy* than in everything that Johnson
wrote. Johnson didn't have the sort of genius for
expression that could discard

> "There scattered oft, the earliest of the year,
>   By hands unseen, are showers of violets found;
> The red-breast loves to build and warble there
>   And little footprints lightly print the ground,"

and leave a poem as great in picturesque beauty
as any in the language. *The Vanity of Human
Wishes*, *Rasselas*, and the essays are not of that
quality. But the point lies somewhere else. The
author of *Rasselas* is, notwithstanding, a greater
man than the author of the *Elegy*. Johnson is
superior to his clothes, to his style, to his works.

He may not be a great literary man and still be a great man in literature.

Johnson lacked art as he lacked personal grace and many other attractive things. He was not a great thinker, and he carried about with him always about as many prejudices as one man has capacity for. He was superstitious and at times ridiculous, but he had a great personality and he had a tremendously great character. That is why people who don't read books by him do read books about him. Boswell's book is one of the world's great books because Johnson is in it, and Johnson's writings are interesting chiefly not because of the artistic beauty in them, but because of the Johnson in them. It isn't so much what he said to his age; it is what he was to his age. What he is speaks so loud that we don't hear what he says. English people love him for his outstanding strength. Character in an heroic and victorious fight with environment is the admirable and universal thing that his life portrays. He is a splendid human document, and it is immensely to the credit of the English people that they have chosen him as one of their great men. Carlyle says eloquently of him: "In his poverty, in his dust and dimness, with the sick body and the rusty coat, he made it do for him, like a brave man. Not wholly without a lodestar in the Eternal; he still had a lodestar, as the brave all need to have; with his eye set on that, he would change his course for nothing in these confused vortices of the lower sea of Time. To the Spirit of Lies bearing death and hunger he could in no wise strike his flag."

It is much the same way with Carlyle. Certain realities of life and fundamentals of character, neglected by his age, he saw and expounded with such force that England, and even the world, was not the same after he had spoken. That he lacked urbanity, lacked graces of personality and conventional graces of style has always been recognized. No misunderstanding on these points has given Carlyle his eminence. The point that must not be lost sight of is this: no English man of letters has surpassed him, if indeed equaled him, in sheer literary power. As a literary man as well as a man in literature he is great.

When Carlyle finished his *French Revolution*, as he started out for a walk in the night, he said to his wife: "I know not whether this book is worth anything, nor what the world will do with it, or misdo, or entirely forbear to do, as is likeliest; but this I could tell the world: You have not had for a hundred years any book that comes more direct and flamingly from the heart of a living man."

It had not. Attempts to pin-pick it with talk of its petty inaccuracies and its "peasant manners" will not avail much. It is not a correct ledger account of the French Revolution. But it is the supreme picture of that "World-Chimæra blowing fire." It is the French Revolution.

In all that Carlyle wrote Carlyle himself is
greatly there. Character and personality are
powerful in what he says beyond the power of any
specific truth that he utters. An age that was sick
recognized in him a great physician: Mr. Chesterton and not Professor Matthews has the true angle
for a view of Carlyle (I do not quote accurately
for I have not the book by me): "He came and
spoke a word and the chatter of rationalism
stopped, and sums would no longer work out and
be ended. He was the breath of Nature turning
in her under the load of civilization, astir in the
very stillness of God to tell us that he was still
there."

Professor Matthews says that Carlyle was out of
sympathy with democracy—yet America was the
first to receive his message as prophetic. He says
that he was out of sympathy with science—yet
Darwin and Huxley both paid tribute to his influence over them. His influence with young men
in every generation since his day has been curiously powerful. One could name a dozen great
men who have testified to the upward impulse he
gave them. There is something elementally
powerful in him. To say that he is not great
because he lacks a certain sort of art is like saying
that the ocean is not great because it is stormy.
One would not discount poise and beauty and
technical perfection, but in a time when leading
critics stand for nothing, when there is so much

ease and beauty in style and nothing else, there seems to be need still that Johnson and Carlyle "be held aloft." The English race would be distinctly poorer if they were blotted from the noble illustrations of its manhood.

HAPPINESS[1]

HAPPINESS is the subject of two interesting books from the October publications. It is a topic that requires a courageous author and only the most serious-minded attempt to expound it. In *The Durable Satisfactions of Life*, Dr. Charles W. Eliot discusses with convincing assurance and sanity, "The Happy Life." He tries to fix once more the erring attention of the world on a few unquestioned verities, and to freshen the old invitations to the open avenues of enduring happiness. Beginning with the lower pleasures, Dr. Eliot does not fail to appreciate the joys of the table. Those who do not get happiness from eating, he says, seldom have much capacity for enjoyment or usefulness of any sort. He would scarcely approve Dr. Johnson's judgment that nothing has been contrived by man which produces so much happiness as a good inn; but is genial enough to hint approval of the reply of the dying old woman to the question of her minister: "Here at the end of a long life, which of the Lord's mercies are you most thankful for?" "My victuals," she said with happy reminiscence. The

[1] From the *North Carolina Review*, November 6, 1910.

eye and ear he next considers as the ready ministers of happiness, and then gives primary emphasis to the domestic affections which he declares
to be "the principle source of happiness and well
being." He then rejects Dr. Oliver Wendell
Holmes's judgment that conversation with quick
minds is one of the few most precious of earth's
general pleasures because this is impossible to
most people. Dr. Eliot substitutes reading. For
this, leisure isn't necessary, money isn't necessary,
only desire and patience. Any life is made worth
living by a happy intercourse with books. To
these aids to happiness Dr. Eliot adds two more:
an attitude of sympathy and helpfulness, and
proper choice of beliefs. "To be of service is a
solid foundation for contentment in this world;
no man can be happy unless the things he chooses
to believe accord with the best in his nature."

The other book attacks the ancient problem
with elaborate scientific analysis. Those persons
who ask for certitude in even so pleasantly un-
certain a matter as happiness will find in Dr. H. S.
Williams's *The Science of Happiness*, a precise
code. A man may learn here with geographical
exactness and latitude and longitude of this elusive phantom. Its absence is due, according to Dr.
Williams, not to a lack of appreciation of books,
but to "an excess of carbohydrates"; what the
unhappy man needs is not "a wee bit ingle" and
a wife, but "a more fundamental ordering of his

volitional inconstancy." "The inherent tendency of the brain centers to operate at the expense of the so-called motor centers," which is the source of his unhappiness, may be regulated as one regulates a steam cock. All of this and much more of the same sort is perhaps scientifically true, and yet an ordinary human being impelled through the warm current of daily affairs by his necessities, affections, and myriad duties and impulses, while admitting that it is true, is impatiently certain that it is not true for him. Happiness is a physiological and scientific certitude only to those who accept life as no more than "a Permanent Possibility of Sensation."

We get some happiness from the belief that this will never do for most of us. All things have two handles; in the matter of happiness the scientific handle is the wrong one. An excess of carbohydrates is no doubt an unhappy condition that may be cured by taking something well shaken before meals, but it does not thereby follow that happiness is its uncertainty. Much of the joy of that inalienable right to its pursuit with which the Declaration declares man to be endowed, comes from the fact that it is merely a pursuit—a sporting proposition with the delightful uncertainty of a game, with fair play and a stout heart as inexorable conditions of success. In fact we not only joyfully discard this doctrine of scientific certainty, but the matter is somewhat pathetically complicated by not knowing that we have it when we get it, and not wanting to know. The bird in the bush is worth two in the hand. Lowell observed that the misfortunes from which we suffer most are those that never come; and a witty Frenchman capped his remark with the comment that we are never so unhappy as we think.

Dr. Dwight's definition of happiness recently quoted by Professor Phelps comes to mind with lively suggestiveness. "The happy man is the man who thinks the most interesting thoughts." This is the definition of an educator, and as suggestive as it is, it has a tinge of class pedantry that limits its truth. One of the most interesting men I ever knew used to wish that he were an empty-headed fool. The fools, he thought, monopolize the fun in life. Hamlet had thoughts of the most vibrant interest, and he attributed his unhappiness to just the fact that his life was "sicklied o'er with the pale cast of thought." Cap and bells are not the symbols of the savant. Happiness doesn't reside in intellectual strength any more than in riches or fame. It doesn't reside in any condition. There is more happiness in getting hold of a particular ten dollars than in owning a million; the happiness of seeing one's name in print may be completely inverted by seeing it misspelled. Nature is too universally fair to restrict happiness to thinkers, or capitalists, or artists, or athletes. It is a by-product of a rightly directed life. It comes most surely when treated as a superfluity. Pursued as a main business it makes life a joke. It comes unsought as the natural consequence of doing right-minded things with rightly directed feelings. The world is too "full of a number of things" for happiness to be limited to a class. It is in this variety of the number of things, trivial and tremendous, deliberate and accidental that we are surprised by our greatest happinesses and even occasionally discover that joy that is the quintessence of happiness—"the happiness that makes the heart afraid."

Marcus Aurelius has a noble paragraph that phrases the doctrine of happiness better than any modern. "If thou workest at that which is before thee, following right reason seriously, vigorously, calmly, without allowing anything else to distract thee, but keeping thy divine part pure, as if thou shouldest be bound to give it back immediately; if thou holdest to this, expecting nothing, fearing nothing, but satisfied with thy present activity according to nature, and with heroic truth in every word and sound which thou utterest, thou wilt live happy, and there is no man who is able to prevent this."

MENTAL EFFICIENCY [1]

THE author of the Book of Proverbs confessed near the end of his collection of great conclusions about the problems of life that there were three or four questions that after all of his thinking still baffled him: "There be three things which are too wonderful for me, yea four which I know not: The way of an eagle in the air; the way of a serpent on a rock; the way of a ship in the midst of the sea, and the way of a man with a maid." Throughout the book he has much to say about a fifth wonder; the way of a man with his mind. Three of these five we have made some progress with. The way of the serpent on the rock is no great mystery to the eye of science; the way of the eagle and the way of the ship we have somewhat compassed; but the way of a man with a maid and the way of a man with his mind are yet uncharted. Mr. Arnold Bennett, the English novelist, in a little book just issued, *Mental Efficiency* (a sort of "How to Get Strong Mentally and How to Stay So"), attacks the last problem with great zest and practical suggestiveness. Why do we spend so much time, he asks, in physical calis-

[1] From the *North Carolina Review*, August 6, 1911.

thenics and so little in mental calisthenics? Why
are we content to let our mental machinery (which
we so greatly value) get rusty and inefficient?
And finally, what are the best ways to attain the
mental efficiency that we readily admit is life's
greatest asset?

Mr. Bennett first considers the causes of our
failure in our previous attempts to be intellectually as strong and active as we feel that we
might be. He assigns three reasons for the failure.
The first is a too heavy program of training as a
beginning. He suggests the reading and re-read-
ing within a specified time of some short but
thoughtful book, such as Spencer's *Education*, and
the making of simple notes within the cover of the
striking thoughts. The second cause of failure is
the ironic smile of less ambitious or less patient
friends. He suggests a careful concealment of our
purpose of mental improvement until we get on
the safe ground of success. The third cause of
failure is neglect to re-arrange the day so as to
provide rigorously for our mental calisthenics.
After these general suggestions Mr. Bennett gives
a definite outline of a few mental exercises. "The
most important preliminary to self-development is
the faculty of concentrating at will." To acquire
this, as a mechanical cure for mental debility, he
advises memorizing twenty lines of great poetry or
prose a week for six months. "Another excellent
exercise is to read a page of no-matter-what, and

16

then immediately to write down—in one's own words or the author's—one's full recollection of it. A quarter of an hour a day. No more. And it works like magic." A third exercise is writing. "I don't care what you write so long as you compose sentences and achieve continuity." A diary he regards as bad, but a journal—notes on whatever of interest one has observed during the day—he thinks is an excellent thing for the average man or woman with a desire to stimulate thinking. "Mental efficiency can be gained by constant practice in meditation—*i. e.*, by concentrating the mind, say, but ten minutes daily, and with absolute regularity on some of the highest thoughts of which it is capable. Failures will be frequent, but they must be regarded with simple indifference and dogged perseverence in the path chosen. If that path be followed without intermission for a few weeks the results will speak for themselves."

These are the suggestions that Mr. Bennett selects from his own thinking and from the suggestions of his correspondents. The last suggestion is an end to be achieved, a luxury of mental efficiency rather than a means of attaining it; for this "concentrating the mind for ten minutes daily on some of the highest thoughts of which one is capable," although it seems simple, is in reality tremendously difficult. First, one must catch his thought, and then endure a fierce fight to hold it—

conquer it. "The hardest task in the world,"
Emerson calls this struggle to think steadily. "I
would put myself in the attitude to look in the
eye an abstract truth," he says in his essay on "In-
tellect", "and I cannot. I blench and withdraw
on this side and on that. I seem to know what he
meant who said, 'No man can see God face to face
and live.' For example, a man intends his mind
without rest in one direction. His best heed long
time avails him nothing. Yet thoughts are float-
ing before him. . . . We say I will walk abroad
and truth will take form and clearness to me. We
go forth, but cannot find it. It seems as if we
needed only the stillness and composed attitude
of the library to seize the thought. But we come
in and are as far from it as at first." Emerson is
dealing here with the relation of the trained mind
to large truth, the menace of defeat that constantly fronts the philosopher whose business is
"meditation on the highest thoughts of which the
mind is capable." But his thought suggests the
experiences of the average man who would like to
be efficient in his mental life, but feels too busy
with his crowded hours of external affairs to endure mental conflicts. In the face of mental problems, small and great, that every day invite us to a
trial of mental strength and mental patience, we
too "blench and withdraw." In fact we are but
cowards when it comes to a straightforward facing
of a ten-round mental fight, and vigorous concen-

tration seems a sort of heroism too exacting to be endured.

The test of mental efficiency for most of us is not in our ability steadily "to meditate on the highest thoughts," but in our ability to bring our mind to bear, up to its fullest capacity, on any thoughts at all; to see and to think through to a clearly finished conclusion the problems that arise in connection with our lives every day. The first and best training ground, therefore, is not Spencer's *Education*, though that, or the like of it, is admirable. We do not need to do new things so much as we need to do the old things in a new way. The difficulty—even with the busiest, is not lack of time nor lack of opportunity for mental development; it is not a question of means, it is a question of use. We read the newspapers and the magazines; we go to church and we go to civic and political meetings; we have our daily work and we have our "evenings off." What relation does our mental machinery bear to our fashion of using these experiences of every day? Rightly used, they make us mentally efficient; wrongly used, they make us mentally dissipated and inefficient. No new and costly apparatus has to be ordered to equip the mental gymnasium. It is already equipped; it may or may not be used.

If one doesn't find a sermon contributing to his spiritual betterment, or a lecture interesting or amusing he need not be bored; and, indifferent, he can make them interesting by making them contribute to his mental betterment by concentrating his mind on what the speaker says, for the purpose of strengthening his attentive and retentive powers. (The worst speakers are best for this purpose.) The value of this exercise may be greatly increased by running over in the mind afterwards the content of the lecture. A further step is to write out a brief synopsis —in connected sentences—of what was said; and a further and final step, to write out a consecutive opinion of what one thinks of what was said. It is better (intellectually speaking) never to hear a sermon or a lecture than to follow the habit of idle semi-listening, with the mind all but submerged under a stream of pleasant imagination, looking into a kaleidoscopic review of broken bits of thoughts and dreams, of pseudo-conversations, mingled with vague regrets at not seeing the coronation, sympathy for the bald spot immediately in front, pleasant recollections of Ty Cobb and hopes that the drought may soon be over. Magazine reading, newspaper reading, novel reading may be done in the same lackadaisical sliding from topic to topic from book to book, or it may be done with intelligent grasp and test of grasp by thoughtful review. Nor is this intelligent method dull and depressingly serious. The fact of the matter is that the finest result of mental confidence and competence is that it makes life interesting.

"That man is happiest who thinks the most interesting thoughts."

When a man is working away at his job, when he is with his friends, when he is quite alone—away from books and the usual apparatus of education—in each of these every-day, all-of-the-time relations he can cultivate the point of view of mental efficiency or of mental indifference; of eager, attentive alertness or sagging mental indolence. "My daily task, that is what mainly educates me." It makes no difference what a man's work is, whether it is sweeping an office or managing one, he can do it with fresh mental application and growth, or he can do it with intellectual absenteeism and depression. Ordinary, every-day sights and experiences are just as naturally mental stimulants as they are mental narcotics. The sight of a falling apple and a steaming kettle may mean nothing or it may mean the law of gravitation and the steam engine. The great problems are not all solved and the key to their solution are in the common experiences of every day. And just as a man can use his work he can use his friends. He can use them as clearing houses of idle gossip and as time-killers, or he can use them and let them use him as a means of thought exchange and mental development. Clubs for discussion are almost unheard of among men outside of colleges and large cities. Yet a man need not be ashamed to expose his thoughts outside of a college, and the men in the small towns have just as much need—perhaps more—for the pleasures and benefits of mental contact and conflict as men in large cities. A club of young men was organized in Atlanta a few days ago. A dozen of them have a simple plan of discussing once a month questions that interest them. It was such a rare thing that the papers gave a sensational amount of space to it.

Whatever the method—and the question is not so much a question of method as of attitude, of patience and of courage—the result should be that we have command over our minds. It isn't a question of thinking greatly; it is a question of thinking efficiently; that is, of getting the best work possible out of the mental machine that we happen to have.

THE NECESSARY MELANCHOLY OF
BACHELORS[1]

"But a man is not truly a bachelor unless he has money," said my niece with a sly little smile.

"Nor is he anything else, unless he has money," I replied more conventionally than sincerely. Then I added, "in these days," to claim the full authority of experience.

"His club, his own little den, the irresponsible enjoyment of his tastes, no life could be more fascinating," continued Alicia, not noticing my poor cynicism. "A real bachelor, though, needs money in plenty. The lacking a wife is merely incidental. A poverty-stricken single gentleman"— she stopped because the thought was unpleasant, and Alicia never indulges her cheerful disposition in the luxury of unpleasant thoughts.

"Further, he needs a sympathetic little niece," I said, yielding to the thought of the days she had made pleasant for me. "It is also well for him to have two maiden aunts to advise regarding investments, and a nephew whom he can advise regarding the conduct of his college course, and

[1] From *Putnam's* and *The Reader*, September, 1908.

248

some married friends of his youth, the patronage of whose wives will teach him humility."

"When he has these, or most of them, he is very comfortable and happy," she said, choosing not to follow my lead.

"When he has these he has comfort, but not happiness," said I, but in soliloquy, for she had turned to the piano. I did not choose, however, to let her soft music woo me from my thoughts.

Comfort is a right fine word, but I am immensely glad that it does not spell happiness. Comfort isn't identical even with content. A very commonplace statement, to be sure; and yet the world goes on the easy assumption that there is a cause-and-effect relation. Bachelors are the best illustration. They are the most comfortable people in the world, and they are assumed to be the happiest. On the contrary, in the typical bachelor there is always a patent vein of melancholy. "Bachelor *equals* jolly good fellow" is miserable arithmetic, the result of crude, superficial observation.

Being a bachelor is a good feeling, a feeling one gloats over in solitude; but a bachelor feels a fundamental lack in the lack of responsible love, and no matter how devil-may-care he may appear, his friends may always see his own consciousness of his lack. It shows itself in a mild melancholy that may not be deeply marked, but that is persistent and clear enough. To the elemental demand for simple and first-hand affection, the best possible response is a strong friendship or two that may be sincere, even beautiful, but that is lacking in a certain necessary vitality. Besides these deep friendships, a bachelor has an assortment of acquaintances, the haphazardness of whose friendship makes him constantly feel how unrelated he is to the real happiness of the world.

To put it more nearly to the liking of the more cynical bachelor, he is touched with melancholy because he has none of the common irritations of family life to keep his mind from his own sweet wrongs. That, at least, is the authorized version of the melancholy of that fine old bachelor, and connoisseur of melancholy, Robert Burton. A great deal of ink has been wasted explaining the exquisite sterility of Thomas Gray. The simple reason lies right here under our hand: he was a bachelor. His most intimate friend, Bonsetten, says that Gray wrote so little because he had not learned through love the fine gift of opening the heart. To say that Gray was a bachelor, and melancholy, and non-productive, is to say the same thing. There are compensations, however. Gray's lugubrious *Elegy* and Burton's *Anatomy of Melancholy* are but a small part of what literature owes to bachelorhood. The melancholy strain is the bachelor strain, although the historians of English literature, assiduous as they are in making subtle syntheses, have not noticed it.

Because it is not subtle at all, but obvious, no doubt. The tender melancholy of Goldsmith is typical of what I mean, rather than that of Cowper or Collins.

Signor Antonio, too, is a case in point of illustration. He felt this necessary oppression of bachelorhood. The cause of his sadness was not that he had drifted into the shadow of impending calamities, as the over-serious critics tell us, nor was it liver complaint, as Booth was wont to say; it was rather the insistent lack of real, vital affection, and its responsibilities. He never felt the sadness of the part he must play so deeply as when he furnished forth his friend to Belmont, though he had no envy and loved Bassanio greatly. And he was even worse off afterwards, without doubt; for he lived under the melancholy assurance that in the household at Belmont he was constantly referred to as "an old dear."

So the world, like a poor relation, accepts the material gifts of bachelors as its due, and then, wise in its own home-sorrow, declares that in spiritual things they are a superficial tribe necessarily. (You recall Lamb's delicate jest about the young married people and the culture of oysters.)

Lord Macaulay was in most respects an ideal bachelor. You find no tears in his life, but no love that makes the heart to burn. He loved his sister's children, and, in bachelor fashion, he romped with them at the house in Ormond Street to the scandal of the neighborhood. He got much joy out of life, and he got success that may be said to be without qualification; but the world has always tried to browbeat his fame, on just this account. A large part of the charge of superficiality that is made against him, is deductive: a man who lived the life he did must have been superficial. That crabbed husband, Carlyle, inspired into superiority by the deepening experience of matrimony, called him "an oatmeal man"; Emerson accused him of interpreting life wholly in terms of material comfort. Carlyle's sneer is altogether unfair, but Emerson's is, after his fashion, near the mark. To the man, when he lives alone, as to the world, the supreme questions of life somehow resolve themselves into this comparatively base question of material comfort.

The bachelorhood of Charles Lamb is quite different. Lamb was, in the real sense, no bachelor at all. The wealth of infinite love he gave to Mary, and the suffering that they endured together put the sanctified touch of hallowed home-life upon his life and upon hers. And then there was the memory of Alice W——.

The cases of Lamb and Macaulay differ because of the different natures of the men, of course, and they differ in the choice and chance of bachelorhood. But do you think that a man is ever a bachelor from cold, deliberate choice? I have put that question to various masculine folk, and have never got a serious affirmative.

Henry, the best of amateur philosophers, in discussing this neglected sociological question with me (thinking, no doubt, that an important decision rested on his answer), diplomatically replied, "Whichever you do, suh, you'll regret it." And this, I take to be the first and final contribution of philosophy, professional or amateur.

However unsatisfactory on the general topic, this remark hints the cause of most bachelorhood: the gentlemen lack the courage of their convictions—though convictions may be a trifle too strong a word. Let us be charitable, therefore, and say that most men drift into bachelorhood, and that many have it thrust upon them. There are many, yes, very many causes. It is seldom the deliberate choice of any man—for which God be thanked.

To which happy conclusion I was led by my gentle niece, who had sat down by my chair, and slipped her hand into mine.